GHOSTS OF THE TRIANGLE

GHOSTS OF THE TRIANGLE

HISTORIC HAUNTS OF RALEIGH, DURHAM AND CHAPEL HILL

RICHARD AND WILLIAM JACKSON

Published by Haunted America

A Division of The History Press

Charleston, SC 29403

www.historypress.net

All images are courtesy of the authors.

First published 2009

Manufactured in the United States

ISBN 978.1.59629.833.0

Library of Congress CIP data applied for.

CONTENTS

CONTENTS

INTRODUCTION

Since the beginning of recorded history, man has written of the afterlife and of those who have returned to walk the earth. North Carolina has a particularly rich history, and along with that history comes the deep-rooted folklore that goes hand-in-hand with historic places. Some of our ghosts are well known around the country, such as the Civil War soldiers that still haunt Fort Macon at Atlantic Beach and Fort Fisher at Kure Beach. There are also the many haunts of Wilmington, along with the infamous "little red man" of Winston-Salem. Asheville has the Pink Lady of the Grove Park Inn, while the mountains have the Brown Mountain lights. All of these stories are famous and are linked to important places in North Carolina. What about the Triangle? Lying quietly in the middle of the state sits the capital city of Raleigh, surrounded by Durham and Chapel Hill.

Growing up in the Triangle and in the South was a unique experience. Religion and folklore walk hand in hand, along with the tradition of storytelling. Sitting on back porches and under shade trees on hot summer evenings as the sun sets, children learn of their roots and their family histories by those who have lived it. On many of these occasions in our youth, there would be a ghost story or two shared by the old folks. These stories were told with the intention of making the young shiver in their Chuck Taylors and lose sleep watching the closet door. We personally believed these stories but never gave them a lot of thought until both of us experienced things that we could not explain.

Prior to these incidents, we would have said that we believed in ghosts—but did we really? More than anything, the experiences made us curious and led us down the path of wanting to know more. We found that through our search for answers about the paranormal we could not help but see the correlation between ghost stories, folklore and history. A ghost is something, or someone, from the past that has passed from this earth and then returned. It's the same for history—history is time that has passed and has come back to us as a memory (or as a class in which we caught up on our sleep in high school). We have found that history and folklore are great companions and that folklore is a great way to make people eager to learn more about the things, places and people around them. We hope that the stories in this book will spark interest in the locations where they take place and that people will become curious about the rich history of the Triangle area.

It is not entirely by accident that this collection of stories came together. Growing up in North Carolina and being students of folklore and ghost stories, we could not have avoided being influenced by the great writers of North Carolina ghost and legends. Authors such as Nancy Roberts, Charles Whedbee and John Harden have all inspired us personally and entertained generations of adults and children alike. We would like to thank these legendary writers for their inspiration, as well as those who have passed on many of these wonderful tales from generation to generation, so that everyone may share the rich history of this great state.

PART I

CHAPEL HILL

The history of Chapel Hill and the history of the University of North Carolina at Chapel Hill are one and the same. In 1789, the North Carolina General Assembly charted the creation of the University of North Carolina, which was to be the first public university to admit students in the United States. The University of Georgia had been chartered by the Georgia General Assembly in 1785 but did not admit students until 1801. Near an old Anglican church, the cornerstone was laid for the East Building on October 12, 1793. In February 1795, a young man named Hinton James, having walked all the way from Wilmington, North Carolina, arrived at the university as its first student. He was alone for two weeks before other students began to arrive. The university grew and prospered over the years and survived the dark days during and after the Civil War. The doors were closed briefly during Reconstruction, due to political and financial strife, but the school survived these times and again reopened its doors to students. In 1932, the process of consolidating the universities in North Carolina into one system began. The system became fully coeducational in 1965, as the Women's College of North Carolina became the University of North Carolina at Greensboro. It was during this period that the

The Old Well on the campus at the University of Chapel Hill.

original campus became known as the University of North Carolina at Chapel Hill.

Today, the school has one of the most beautiful campuses in the United States and boasts traditions that rival any other university in the nation. The campus at UNC is made up of quads, the two main being Polk Place and the "Pit." Polk Place is named after President James K. Polk, who was a native of North Carolina and an alumnus of the university. The Pit does not have a great namesake, but it is the central part of the campus for the students. The bookstore and dining halls are located at the Pit, and it is close to the library. When the weather is nice, the Pit becomes a melting pot of students, talking and relaxing during the time that one could only hope is between classes.

Close to this hot spot, across the street between the Pit and Keenan Stadium, where the Carolina football team plays, is the Morehead-

Patterson Bell Tower. The bell tower is a stunning sight, especially in the fall as the sun slowly sets, and the tower is illuminated against the autumn sky. Across the campus, between the Old East and Old West Buildings, is the Old Well. Modeled after the Temple of Love in the Garden of Versailles, the Old Well was built on the spot of the original working well at the university. It is said that if incoming freshmen drink from the well, they will receive straight As for their first semester of classes. This myth can be discredited by an ungodly number of people. Across McCorkle Place, near the infamous Franklin Street—the staging ground for the many celebrations for national titles and other big basketball game victories—stands the most controversial student at the school. Silent Sam is a monument that was built to honor the many young men that left the school to fight in the Civil War. Some argue that the statue represents the fight to uphold the practice of slavery, but supporters of the statue say that Silent Sam represents those who, as in most wars, did not make the policies or start the war but were drafted to fight in it.

The university has many traditions, such as the Halloween celebration that takes place on Franklin Street every year and draws the most charming people imaginable to the party. The sports traditions are the most famous for the university and, again, are comparable to any other university in the United States. The football team has a long-standing rivalry with the University of Virginia, which dates back to the creation of the football teams at both schools. In more recent history, this rivalry has been overshadowed by UNC's football rivalry with North Carolina State University, which is located right down the road in Raleigh. UNC's biggest rivalry, however, is on the hardwood with the Duke University Blue Devils of Durham, which is even closer than Raleigh. These two basketball powerhouses are located roughly eight miles apart and play at least twice a year. These games for fans of both schools are like the Super Bowl, Christmas and a trip to the dentist wrapped up in one. The games always prove to be close contests that are rarely decided before the final seconds, and losing could mean prodding by co-workers or friends from the time of the game until the next meeting.

In concluding this brief history of UNC, there only remains one question: what the hell is a "Tar Heel"? The answer is in legend rather than historical fact. Sometime during the Civil War (or, as sometimes told, the Revolutionary War), the soldiers from North Carolina were joshing the soldiers from Virginia about their inadequacy on the field of battle, when one of the Virginians stated that the North Carolinians needed to get some tar and put it on the bottoms of their shoes to help them to stick in battle instead of running away from the fight. The name, too, stuck and naturally was carried back to the place that represents the state that the men called home.

Because of its beauty, mystique and tradition, the University of North Carolina is a place where anyone who attends the school or lives in Chapel Hill would want to stay forever. It appears that some poor souls did, in fact, decide to spend eternity there. There are many stories and legends of ghosts in Chapel Hill. The unusal thing about the stories that are heard and passed down in a university town is that we will never know how much of the story is true and how much of the story is just urban legend handed down through generations of students. Either way, the stories are entertaining and certainly help to carry on the tradition of Chapel Hill.

The Horace Williams House

The Horace Williams House in Chapel Hill is owned today by the Preservation Society of Chapel Hill, and it serves as its headquarters. The house has gone through many changes and renovations over the years. The oldest part of the house is the dining room, or the farmhouse room, as it is sometimes called, which was built in the 1840s. The property, along with the house, was purchased from the university for $300 in 1855 by a chemistry professor named Benjamin S. Hedrick. During the time that Hedrick owned the house, he added on what would come to be known as the octagon room. Built sometime between 1852 and 1855, the room is connected to the original part of the house by a breezeway that makes the house unique. Hedrick was criticized and finally dismissed from the university for his political view on slavery and for his support of John C. Fremont, a radical Republican presidential candidate who opposed slavery. After his dismissal, Hedrick left the state and sold the house to H. Hosea Smith for $1,500.

Smith was a Northerner and was also unpopular among faculty and students for refusing to volunteer for the Confederate army during the Civil War. Students once even set off a powder charge under his seat during class. During the time that Smith occupied the house, he was frequently visited by Governor Zebulon Vance. Smith sold the house in 1879 to a professor of Latin named George T. Winston for $1,000. During the time that Winston lived in the house, he made many additions and changes, such as the front porch, the front parlor and the enclosure of the entrance hall. He served as university president from 1891 to 1896,

The parlor of the Horace Williams House, showing the portrait of the professor hanging over the fireplace.

View from the front of the Horace Williams House.

when he left to become the president of the University of Texas. Later, he returned to North Carolina to become the second president at North Carolina State University in Raleigh. In 1891, when Winston became president at UNC, the house's namesake took up residence.

Horace Williams was a graduate of the university, and upon receiving his doctorate in divinity from Yale, he was appointed as the chair of the Mental Health and Moral Science Department at UNC. For almost fifty years, Williams stayed at the university and became incredibly popular among the student population for his teaching style. He preferred to use open discussion rather than just lecture. When Horace Williams died in 1940, he left the house to the university, which used it as a rental for professors until it was finally taken over by the Preservation Society.

Many people believe that Horace Williams never left the house at all. It has been reported over the years that the fireplace tools will move from one side of the fireplace to the other at night. Children who have lived in the house have said that they have seen the ghost of Horace Williams—and not only have they seen him, but they also have held conversations with him. One caretaker reported that a rocking chair in the house will sometimes begin to rock on its own. All of the reports about the disturbances tell of a friendly presence, nothing menacing. The house has been investigated many times, but no solid evidence has ever been obtained to substantiate the claims. The house, located at 610 East Rosemary Street, remains open to the public, and even without a "smoking gun" of paranormal activity, the house remains a landmark of the rich history of Chapel Hill and a magnet for ghost hunters of all degrees.

If you visit the house, take the time to look up at the large portrait of Horace Williams in the front room. Chills will go down your spine, as the professor's face gives out an extremely personal and human quality. The portrait looks down at you and gives you a sense that you may be looking at someone you once knew—a lost friend or family member that you remember from childhood. He can easily be imagined living and teaching in Chapel Hill, which only makes the stories of his spirit inhabiting the grounds more eerie.

The Legend of Peter Droomgoole

The legend of young Peter Droomgoole is an essential part of any historic analysis of Chapel Hill. The story has been retold many times and has many versions, but they are all very similar. The legend tells of eighteen-year-old Peter Droomgoole arriving in Chapel Hill about 1830 to attend the university. He was a high-strung young man who enjoyed drinking, playing cards and womanizing. Soon after he arrived, he became smitten with a beautiful young woman named Fanny. Peter soon gave up his extravagant ways and became totally devoted to Fanny. They would meet every evening around dusk at a high point on the east side of Chapel Hill, a spot called Piney Prospect. There on the rocks, they would stay for hours and talk about a future together, as young lovers are known to do. As their relationship progressed, another student became enamored of Fanny and goaded Peter about his love. Pride overtook Peter, and he challenged the man to a duel. Although dueling had been outlawed in North Carolina in 1802, it was still considered an appropriate way for a man to reclaim his honor and dignity.

The other man accepted, and they met at Piney Prospect with their seconds on a foggy fall morning. The two men stood back to back and began to count off paces. As they turned and fired, Fanny appeared on the scene, having been warned of the duel by a friend. She screamed in horror as Peter dropped his pistol and crumpled to the ground. She rushed to his side and held him in her arms as he died. The young men quickly quieted Fanny and set about burying Peter in a shallow grave on the hillside. The parties involved went their separate ways to hide their involvement in Peter's death. Fanny, heartbroken, left school but returned periodically to Piney Prospect over the years to mourn her lover and to think of all of the dreams they'd had that would never come true. She died a few years after the duel, some say of a broken heart, having always felt responsible for Peter's dying in defending her honor.

Peter's family became extremely worried after months of no communication from him, and his uncle, a Virginia congressman, came to Chapel Hill to find out what had happened to his nephew. There were reports that Peter had left to go to Europe to travel the Continent but never came back. There were also rumors that he had joined the army and ended up out West, later getting killed in a gunfight, but the congressman never came to the truth about Peter. He remained an open wound to his family for generations. To this day, it is said that Peter returns to Piney Prospect to search for Fanny, and it is also reported that Fanny can be seen there sitting on the rocks, reminiscing and waiting for her lover. Some have even reported that there are rocks at Piney Prospect that have strange brownish-red stains on them that seem to bleed during rainstorms.

The legend of Peter Droomgoole has stood the test of time, not only due to the fascinating story itself but because of the magnificent

Gimghoul Castle that was built on the site in 1926. The castle was originally named Hippol Castle and was built by the Order of the Gimghouls, a society that was formed by university students who had heard the legend and formed a fraternity for juniors and seniors based on the story of Peter Droomgoole. The castle is said to be haunted, and a dark hooded figure looms in the window of the south room, facing the reported spot of the duel, pointing out. Is this Peter, or maybe his killer, trapped in this spot, waiting for eternity to catch up to him? The castle is an amazing architectural feat, but it is still owned by the society, and "No Trespassing" signs are posted all over the property. It is not suggested that anyone go there "ghost hunting," as many people have been escorted off of the property by the authorities in the past for trespassing.

The Carolina Inn

The Carolina Inn was built in 1924 to accommodate visitors to the University of North Carolina. In 1920, there were very few places for visitors of the university to stay, and in November 1921, the famous University Inn burned down. John Sprunt Hill, a UNC graduate, decided that he would build a hotel that would house the professors and alumni who frequented the university. The hotel was built at the site of the eighteenth-century New Hope Chapel, for which Chapel Hill was named. The structure was modeled after the Potomac side of George Washington's home at Mount Vernon. In 1935, Hill left the hotel to the university, with the stipulation that the profits from the deed would go to funding the library system of the university. The Carolina Inn has hosted many famous dignitaries, intellectuals and stars over the years. One of the most famous of these visitors was North Carolina's own Andy Griffith, who as a young actor, just starting out, performed his stand-up monologue "What It Was, Was Football." Another now-famous occupant of the hotel was Dr. William Jacocks, a physician with the International Health Division of the Rockefeller Foundation. Dr. Jacocks lived in the

The Carolina Inn in Chapel Hill has been a mainstay in Chapel Hill since 1924.

inn between 1948 and 1965 in suite number 252, and some claim that he never left.

Although Jacocks died in Burke County and not the hotel itself, he is rumored to still occupy this area of the hotel. His spirit is not considered to be malicious in any way, and as a matter of fact, his spirit is described as more of a prankster. One of the spirit's favorite tricks is to lock the guests out of their rooms from the inside. Even after the $16.5 million renovation and modernization in 1996, the doctor was not dissuaded. He still locks the rooms, with a disregard for the new, modern electronic key cards now used as room keys. On some occasions, maintenance has had to be called to enter the room with a ladder from the window over the door. It is still reported that items are moved and doors closed in the rooms of the suite. Guests and employees have heard music in the rooms. The visitors and employees all seem not to mind the presence and feel

Does the Carolina Inn have a permanent guest?

that it is a lighthearted entity that enjoyed life and wants to enjoy the afterlife just as much.

Those who have close ties to the inn believe that Dr. Jacocks enjoyed the inn so much that he returned to spend eternity there. The Carolina Inn today is still an important historic feature of Chapel Hill, and it is more than just a hotel where visitors come to sleep. Today, the inn provides a comfortable place to stay, along with a wonderful history to enjoy.

Memorial Hall

The original Memorial Hall was built in 1885. The hall was the first building erected after the university reopened in 1875, having closed its doors due to the hardships that befell the university after the Civil War. During the war, the university lost a substantial number of students, even though the president of the university, David L. Swain, petitioned Jefferson Davis in 1861 to allow an exemption from the war for students. The Confederate president had allowed it, but in 1864 Secretary of War James Seddon revoked the exemption for freshmen and sophomores. These young men were called to fight in a war that many of them had gone to school to avoid, and many never came home. After the war, Swain did all he could to keep the university open, but with depleted enrollment, increasing debts and a rising public anger toward Swain for working with the Reconstruction government, he was forced to tender his resignation. New president Solomon Pool soon found out that he would face the same problems as his predecessor. Low enrollment, little financial support and anti-Republican sentiments caused the university to shut its doors in 1871.

A ghostly spectator has been known to watch the shows at Memorial Hall.

After the school reopened, it became apparent that the dated Gerrard Hall could no longer meet the school's needs. Plans were laid to erect a new building in honor of David Swain and other North Carolinians who had worked so hard for the university during the Civil War. The hall was built and served the university until the late 1920s, when again, due to the growth in Chapel Hill, it became necessary to tear the building down and rebuild another Memorial Hall on the site of the original. In the new and improved Memorial Hall, 160 marble plaques commemorating Swain and others were installed. Since the new building has been in existence, there have been rumors of paranormal activity. Some people claim to have seen a lone man sitting in the middle of the theatre; others claim to have heard voices in the corridors of Memorial Hall. The spirit is not described as a friendly presence but rather as a foreboding ghoul that is very frightening. Aside from these feelings that people get in the spirit's presence, the ghostly man is not mischievous and hardly ever bothers anyone. At times, he definitely tries to get the attention of an unlucky visitor or employee, but he rarely makes his presence known. When he does appear, he silently watches a performance and fills the room with a sense of dread and sadness. It has become tradition that a seat is saved for the resident spirit at every show, but it's not known if he attends all of the shows or if he is choosey about the performances he attends. It is possible that the spirit is just a holdover from the rich history of the original building, but regardless of the truth of the matter, the stories add to the legend and ambiance of the theatre.

Caldwell Hall

Another famous building at the University of North Carolina at Chapel Hill is Caldwell Hall, which houses the philosophy department. Caldwell, at one point, housed the medical school for the university and was the home of the medical library at UNC. For decades, the building was where Horace Williams went to work every day. The professor was loved by his students and truly loved teaching and expanding young minds. When he died, there was a void left in the building and an emptiness in the classrooms and corridors of Caldwell Hall. Since his death, that void has sometimes been filled with a familiar presence.

It is said that the ghostly figure of a man—which fits Williams's description as a slim man with glasses—can still be seen walking the halls. Many times a student or a professor will be passing through the halls, and pass a tall, skinny man wearing glasses. As they pass the man they smile, a feeling of familiarity will overtake them and they will stop and turn to try to take another look at him to figure out where they had seen him before. When they turn, they find themselves alone in the long hallway. The face that they saw will not come to them until later most times, or sometimes when they are standing in the Horace Williams House staring up at the portrait of the man himself. As they peer into his face, they remember the face they saw at Caldwell Hall that stirred such familiarity.

Many times a professor or student will find themselves working late at Caldwell, and they will experience the feeling of not being alone in an empty room. Could the professor possibly be just as busy in death as he was in life? Can the ghost of a departed soul haunt more than one place at a time, or is this a phantom that appears as a picture in time of Horace Williams hard at work preparing a lesson to educate his students? One thing is for sure: wherever the professor's presence is felt, it is not a feeling of dread or sorrow, but rather a positive energy of warmth and familiarity. Horace Williams was perhaps one of the greatest educators in the history of the state of North Carolina; his tireless devotion to his students may continue to this day as his spirit is by far the busiest spirit in Chapel Hill.

The Forest Theatre

Kemp Plummer Battle was born in 1831 and entered the University of North Carolina in 1845. He graduated as the valedictorian of his class and spent the next few years tutoring Latin and mathematics at the university while he worked on his law degree. Battle passed the North

Carolina Bar in 1854 and practiced in Raleigh. He returned to the university as a trustee in 1862 only to be removed six years later by the Reconstruction General Assembly. His removal served as punishment for his loyalty to the Confederacy during the Civil War. Battle was not done with the University of North Carolina, though, and returned in 1874 to regain his stature as a trustee, then as the university president in 1876. He served in this role until 1891 and then retired as an alumni history professor. The remainder of Battle's life was spent compiling his two-volume *History of the University of North Carolina*, as well as preserving the forest at the heart of Chapel Hill that he so dearly loved.

Battle wrote of his time at the university spent in the forest and, in particular, his preparation for his valedictory that he delivered when he graduated. Battle recalled how he practiced his speech there in the forest in front of the rocks and trees and made ready for his big moment in the spotlight. During his time as president, he set aside the land and began to build trails through the beautiful woods. The Forest Theatre at Battle Park was first used for theatrics in 1916, and in 1919 the site of an outdoor theatre was decided upon. The outdoor theatre was built using Work Projects Administration funds and was based on the Manteo and Williamsburg, Virginia theatres that were designed by Albert Bell. The first organized outdoor performance was held in 1951, but ever since 1940, when the construction of the outdoor theatre began, there have been reports of a presence on stage. Many people passing by the theatre in Battle Forest or even later on near Country Club Road have reported hearing the sounds of passionate acting taking place on the stage. As they draw near to see what performance is taking place or to spy on a rehearsal by local actors preparing for a show, they find that the stage is empty, and the voices dissipate into the breeze as if they were never there. Sometimes, a bigger surprise waits for those curious passersby. There have been some reports of a green, glowing figure standing in the center of the theatre that disappears before their eyes. The figure stands on stage as if it is about to perform an act for an unseen audience. Could this be a former tragic young actor or actress that once appeared onstage there returning for an encore? Or could it be Kemp Battle returning to a beloved place in his afterlife, practicing his speech once more?

The Forest Theatre at Battle Park is the stage on which phantom actors perform.

The DuBose House

On the outskirts of town is a new, upscale development called Meadowmont. At the center of this area lies the Paul J. Rizzo Conference Center, which serves as an integral part of the Kenan-Flagler Business School. At this location stands the historic DuBose House, which was built in 1933 by David St. Pierre DuBose and his wife, Valinda Hill DuBose. Mr. DuBose was a 1921 graduate of the University of North Carolina, majoring in electrical engineering. He worked from 1922 until the early 1930s in Baltimore, Maryland, for the Consolidated Gas and Electric Company. When his first child was born, DuBose decided to move his family back to Chapel Hill and create a rural estate that the family could share. DuBose purchased a tract of land that had once been part of the first land grant to William Barbee of Middlesex, Virginia. He had received the land from the Earl of Granville, and much of this original tract became the ground that the University of North Carolina stands on today.

When the house was completed, it was breathtaking. The DuBose house was a twenty-thousand-square-foot Georgia Revival–style home that to this day stands out in local architecture. Wood from the original homeplace of William Barbee was milled and carved to create the paneling in the new house. Valinda DuBose looked at her house sitting on a hill, surrounded by rolling meadows, and immediately dubbed the house Meadowmont, the name that the grounds still carry today. Before her death in 1989, she asked that the house, along with twenty-eight acres, be bequeathed to the university one day, and the house remained the DuBose family home until St. Pierre's death in 1994. The university decided to use the land to develop the Paul J. Rizzo Conference Center, and today the house is used for dining and social events. Many times in the beautiful DuBose House, an unsettling or uncomfortable feeling will engulf guests. The feeling is out of place in the grand house, but many who have felt it would say that in a crowded room of young professionals they sometimes feel alone, and a sense of dread overtakes them. Other people claim that sometimes, out of the corner of their eye, they will see someone enter a room or walk past a door, but when they turn to look no one is there. Does the DuBose House remain a family home to the ones passed who so enjoyed their lives there, or could it even be the spirit of William Barbee still wandering the grounds so many years after his death?

PART II

DURHAM

Durham did not officially exist as a city until 1869 and not as a county until 1881, but its history dates back farther as a community and a place of expansion and growth in the state. The area was first settled about 1750 in the low grounds along the Eno, Flat and Little Rivers. These areas provided abundant game, fertile soil for farming and water power for the gristmills that were necessary for the growth of the community. The gristmills represented a booming industry in the region. Located along the rivers in the area, they helped to bring prosperity to some of the early families of the region, such as the McCown, Cabe, Sim, Bennehan and Cameron families. In 1853, a rail station was established between the areas known as Pinhook, which is modern-day west Durham, and Prattsburg, which is located near Edgemont or present-day east Durham. The station was named after a local doctor, Bartlett S. Durham, a country physician who sold the four acres to the railway company for the building's construction. Though Durham was an established community after the formation of the rail station, the real boom came after the Civil War with the high demand for bright leaf tobacco that the Union and Confederate soldiers had become accustomed to while in the area during the surrender of Confederate general Joseph Johnston to Union general William Sherman at the Bennett Farm. Capitalizing on this demand, the

A replica of the Old Bull Durham Sign located at the Durham Bulls Athletic Park.

Duke family also became the dominant force in post–Civil War Durham, contributing to the tobacco and textile industry and also providing endowments for hospitals, such as Watts, and Trinity College, which would later become Duke University.

African Americans had many opportunities in Durham that were not available in other parts of the South. By the early 1900s, Durham was home to the National Religious Training School at Chatauqua (present-day North Carolina Central University), Lincoln Hospital and North Carolina Mutual Life Insurance Company, which was to become the largest black-owned financial institution in the world. At this time in Durham's history, Parrish Street was known as "Black Wall Street." With the rich history of Durham, it is no wonder that there are many unexplained sightings and phenomena. Although the tobacco factories and textiles are gone, replaced now by the sprawling Research Triangle

Park, the buildings of days gone by remain, along with the beautiful preserved areas and parks, such as the Eno River, Stagville Preservation Center, Duke Homestead and West Point on the Eno. Walking through these tranquil sites transports you back to a different time and place—and possibly acts as a portal to see things that are not supposed to be seen. And if you are lucky, you may catch a glimpse of one of the past residents of this colorful city. Today, Durham stands as one of the most diverse cities in the nation. The City of Medicine, as Durham is called, is a beacon for research, culture and entertainment. Durham is the home to the Duke University Blue Devils, who are participants in one of the greatest rivalries in college basketball, and the Durham Bulls, a Triple A baseball team that was made famous by the movie *Bull Durham*.

Watts Hospital

Watts Hospital originally opened in February 1895 as a gift from George Washington Watts. The hospital was a wooden structure, located on the corner of Main and Buchanan Streets in Durham. The original hospital was composed of four buildings, connected to one another by breezeways or corridors. By 1906, the hospital was already in need of more room, due to the steady increase in population of the growing town. The present location on Broad Street, in Durham, was completed and opened to the public in May 1909 and served citizens of Durham until the new Durham County Hospital opened in 1976. In the sixty-seven years that the hospital was in operation, the walls of the building saw much death and suffering, but they also saw the happiness and joy of parents seeing their newborn children for the first time. With all of the emotion contained in these walls, it is no wonder that there is so much activity reported. Since 1980, the hospital has been home to the North Carolina School of Science and Mathematics. The school today bustles with students, faculty and, at times, with the spirits of patients who never left.

Front view of the old Watts Hospital buildings.

There have been numerous reports of laughter throughout the hallways and giggles of little girls playing hide-and-seek in the empty halls. Cries of infants can still be heard near the nursery, and in the halls that once served as the morgue the doors are known to close on their own, while water faucets turn on by themselves in the dead of night. One interesting story, told by one of the school's longtime security employees, involves a late-night encounter with what may possibly have been the spirit of a nurse who was murdered in the 1960s. One night, it was raining harder than the security guard had ever seen it rain. He sat restlessly in his car, watching out over the campus for anything out of the ordinary, when he noticed two white spots moving between two buildings. He watched the spots curiously pass each other, back and forth, until they got close enough to see that the spots were a lady's shoes. The woman walked briskly through the rain, with her head down and her hair covering her face. She clutched a sweater tightly around her neck and wore a knee-length white dress.

The guard figured it was just someone who had been out all night partying and was crossing the campus on her way home. He put the car in drive and pulled out slowly to meet her to see if she was okay or needed any help. He pulled his car abreast of her and cracked his window. "Are you okay?" he asked. He's said that he will never forget the next few moments until the day he dies. The woman stopped suddenly, as if she was taken by surprise by his presence, and slowly—very slowly— she turned her head toward the car. Her face was pale, and the water ran down her stringy hair across her face. She spoke in a voice that seemed not right for this world. "No, I'm on my way home," she said and slowly turned her head back down and began to walk away. He sat still, momentarily shocked as she walked away from the car, and he realized that something was not right. He turned the car and began to follow her to make sure that she made it off campus all right.

She turned the corner at the gymnasium, and he immediately turned after her. But to his surprise, no one was there. He jumped out of his car, knowing that the only place she could have gone was through a side door into the gym. He jerked on the doors, but they were locked. He

Watt's Hospital is now the home of the North Carolina School of Science and Mathematics.

fumbled for his keys and then opened the door. To his surprise, there was no sign of anyone having entered the gym. The floor was completely dry; there was no mud, no footprints. Where could she have gone? He knew that there was nowhere else she could have gone. As he relocked the door, the thought came to him that maybe she was not just a local crossing the campus. He remembered that in the 1960s, there had been a nursing student at the hospital who had gone out on a date and had never returned. Her body had been found in a rural area, and to this day, the murder is unsolved.

Could this have been that young nursing student trying in vain to get home? He doesn't know the answer to that question, but he knows that what he saw cannot be explained away. He knows also that many nights he has played hide-and-seek in the building where the old morgue was with a giggling girl, when no one else has been in the building. He would hear her around a corner and run as fast as he could to catch a glimpse of her. When he rounded the corner, there would be emptiness and only the sound of laughter echoing down the hall. After many years of working at the school, he reflects: "When you've been here so many years, working late nights and holidays, with no one in the buildings but you, you've got to make the best of it. There have been many nights when I've walked down these halls during violent thunderstorms, with rain pounding against the old hospital windows, and [I've] recited the Lord's Prayer as a comfort to myself and, hopefully, to any of the restless spirits that hear me." There have been numerous reports of unexplained sights and sounds at the school. The occurrences have not been limited to just one person, so the question of one guard's sanity has not been an issue. For now, the faculty and students continue to coexist with the spirits of the old hospital and, in some cases, even embrace their presence as a window into the past.

Cabe Family Cemetery

Among some of the earliest settlers to the area that is now known as Durham were the mill owners of the Eno Flat River. These families became the elite of Durham at the time, due to the fact that they were ambitious and hardworking. Prosperity followed these families and their community, as they invested in land and business ventures in the area. To assure the longevity of their success, these families became extremely close and practiced intermarrying. One of these families was the Cabe family. The patriarch of this family was Squire John Cabe, who owned a mill along the Eno and several others in the region. The squire had three wives over the course of his life and nine daughters. He had no sons to carry on his legacy, but he made sure that his daughters were taken care of. One of his daughters, Rachel, was married into the McCown family, another prosperous family of the area. She helped her husband, Moses, run a mill that was located on the present-day site of Cole Mill Road and the Eno, where the original dam can still be seen. John Cabe wanted to keep his family together, even in death, so he established the Cabe Family Cemetery.

Accessed off of Sporger Road in Durham, the cemetery is approximately a quarter-mile through the woods down a trail. Around the cemetery are many other hiking trails and forests. The cemetery is surrounded by peaceful and majestic hardwoods that provide a canopy from the sun and sky. As people walk along the bluffs and hills, they may come across this lonely cemetery. Walking past the rows of headstones, people can see the graves of John Cabe, Rachel and other members of the Cabe and the McCown families. The serenity of the woods does not spill into the cemetery, though, as there exists a feeling of uneasiness there. Children crying, laughter and the feeling of being watched are often reported by those who've been there. Many would-be "ghost seekers" have had experiences in the cemetery that have been described as emotionally draining, and many have said that they would never return to the place, "especially at dusk," as one woman put it. Much of the activity in the cemetery seems to focus around a prominent granite stone in the center of the cemetery. It has been reported that around the stone, one can always feel "cold spots," which tend to move but stay in proximity to the stone. The stone marks the grave of Moses Ellis McCown, an early mayor of Durham.

Two men visited the site in search of ghosts one spring day and found what they were looking for. Around the Moses Ellis McCown stone, they found the moving "cold spots" of which they had heard reports. The day was warm, but the two men could put their hands in the spot that was as cold as a refrigerator. The drop in temperature was drastic and moved around the stone, up and down and back and forth. Another visitor to the site stood on the bluff, looking down at the cemetery. He walked slowly through the cemetery, alone, looking at the stones and reading the names. Suddenly, he felt that he was not really alone. He looked around through the trees for his unseen stalker, but no one was there. The feeling became so intense that he hurriedly left the area. Was this feeling just a figment of an overactive imagination? If there is a presence there, why is it so restless? We will probably never know the answer to that question. It is best to just leave the little plot of ground to the Cabe family, where they remain as close in death as they were in life.

The Haunted Farmhouse

Built around the turn of the twentieth century, the two-story white farmhouse stands on a hill surrounded by century-old majestic oak trees that overlook the beautiful, untouched countryside of Durham County. The home and property have had many owners over the years, and it is evened rumored that during Prohibition the home served as a place where one could obtain a drink of illegal corn liquor, or "moonshine," as some would call it. The present owners, who have owned the house for more than twenty years, have found possible evidence of past violence in the house. While renovating in the late 1980s and tearing down an interior downstairs wall, .38-caliber bullets were found imbedded in a stud. The bullets had been fired from the inside of the house and not from the outside. Did acts of unspeakable violence occur within the walls of the old farmhouse? Do those who lived, worked and died in the house remain?

The present owners of the house began noticing strange happenings during the renovation of the old place. Strange smells would often permeate the air—a smell of dirt and body odor, as if someone who had just put in a hard day's work in the field walked by, unseen to the human eye. The renovation period was also when the first apparition was seen. The owners, along with an electrician who had just finished with the electrical upgrades in the home, were standing in the driveway after a long afternoon of work. The electrician made a comment about the young man who was looking down at them from the upstairs window. The owner glanced up at the figure and assumed that his son had remained inside the house when everyone else had left. The men said goodbye,

The old farmhouse in which a shadowy figure has been seen looking from the upstairs window.

and the owner went inside the house to get the boy and go home. He stood at the bottom of the stairs and called the boy's name several times. Frustrated by the lack of an answer to his calls, he finally bounded up the stairs to get his son. As he searched the second floor, he realized that he was alone. He left for the day, and upon arriving at his home, he discovered that his son had been there for the past three hours, having left earlier with some of the other family members.

When the family finally moved into the house, things became worse. On frequent occasions, the parents, who slept downstairs, would be awakened by loud noises and banging upstairs in the room that their two sons occupied. Angry, they would go upstairs to see what was going on, and they would find the two boys sleeping, unaware of any disturbance. The noises became routine and were largely overlooked by the family, but it was terrifying to guests who visited the house. During the early years in the house, two of the family members again encountered a full-bodied apparition. The first was seen by the father while he was making lunch in the kitchen one afternoon. He was standing at the stove, cooking, when he saw what he describes as a "grayish figure, walking almost in slow motion" move across the room from the living room hallway, across the kitchen and through the wall. Interestingly, where the apparition walked through the wall was the original location of the door that led to the backyard, before the renovation of the house. When the house was remodeled, the door was replaced by a wall, to make room for an extension to the house. Was this the same figure who had peered down from the second story years before? The second apparition that was seen in the house was that of a female.

Late one night, the family was awakened by the terrified screams of the sister, who also slept upstairs. The family rushed in to make sure she was all right, and when she was finally calmed, she told what happened. She woke up in the middle of the night and realized that the room was extremely cold. She reached out for her blanket to cover herself and realized that it was gone. When she couldn't find her covers, she opened her eyes and through the dim light coming into the room from the hallway, she could see a woman in her room, wearing a white gown. She assumed it was her mother and sat up in the bed to speak to her. As her eyes focused, she realized that it was not her mother, and terrified at the presence, she covered her eyes and began to scream. When the family came in there was no one in the room with the girl, but she remained shaken for a long time. The blanket that had covered her when she went to bed was across the room, draped over a dollhouse, as if it had levitated perfectly across the room and dropped straight down over the dollhouse.

One of the most frightening events in the house took place just a few years ago, when the oldest son returned to the house with his wife and two young daughters to housesit for his parents while they were on vacation. His wife put the girls to bed and returned downstairs to where she and her husband would spend the night. As the young couple relaxed, the conversation turned to the spirits that inhabited the house. The young wife scoffed at the idea of ghosts and that the house was haunted, but as she was making a taunting comment to her husband about the ghosts, the downstairs door suddenly slammed shut. No one was near the door, but it closed as if pushed by an invisible force. They looked at each other and decided that the conversation was best suited for another time and prepared for bed. As they turned off the lights and lay down to sleep, the mother's concern turned to the girls, who might possibly wake up in the night and fall down the narrow staircase. Her husband reassured her that they were fine and that they would be all right sleeping upstairs. No sooner had they relaxed and tried to sleep than the silent darkness erupted into banging and thudding, as if someone was falling down the stairs. They both heard it, and without a word they leapt out of bed, turned on the light and rushed to the bottom of the stairs. Nothing was found there but emptiness, though the family's two dogs stared at the spot, growling, with fur standing on end. The husband rushed upstairs and found his daughters asleep. He woke them up and brought them downstairs to sleep with them for the rest of the night. "What frightened me most," the wife later said, "was that it was almost as if the ghost was listening to us and purposely played that prank on us, feeding off of the fear we had for our children's falling down the stairs."

Even with such disturbances, the same family has owned and occupied the house for years, and they are not about to let anything run them away. There are still noises in the night, doors that close and the sounds of furniture being moved in the upstairs bedrooms. "But that's not enough to make us leave," the owner says. "I've dreamed of owning that place since I was a child, and it's going to take a lot more than that to run us out of our home." The home is located off of Wake Forest Road in Durham and is a private residence.

Country Church

Located on a two-lane road outside of the city is a small, white country church that is reported to be haunted. The church sits amid green rolling hills and tall North Carolina pine trees. The church and the surrounding area are almost out of place in the growing region. To think about a church as being haunted is unsettling, but events that have been reported in the small structure leave many unanswered questions. The structure of the church itself was built around the 1960s, and the present congregation moved into the church during the 1970s after their original church was destroyed in a fire. Many people have reported seeing a little boy inside the church at times when no one should be there. The occurrences have become a part of the church, and the congregation has affectionately named the boy Luke.

There are no details known about Luke or who he is. The only thing that is known is that he enjoys playing in the sanctuary of the church. Several years ago, the fire marshal came to the church to do his regular inspection of the building. As he approached the glass doors that serve as the entrance to the church, he could see a small boy playing in the middle of the aisle. He cupped his hands against the glass and looked into the church. There was only the little boy and no sign of any adults. He tapped on the glass, and the boy looked up in surprise. Seeming frightened, the child ran and hid out of sight of the fire marshal. The fire marshal tapped on the glass again in an attempt to coax the boy out of hiding, but to no avail. He stepped back and realized that there was only his car in the parking lot, and as he walked around the church, he also noticed that all of the doors were locked. He was convinced that a homeless family had broken into the church and was using the facility during the week. As he stood in the parking lot, pondering the situation, the pastor arrived with the keys. The fire marshal told the pastor about what had happened, and they began to search the church from top to bottom. There was no one inside the church, and all of the doors were still locked from the inside. Who is this little boy who is so elusive? Who is Luke? Whoever he is, the parishioners claim to hear sounds of movement coming from the basement of the church. They sometimes feel as if they are being watched and hear the sounds of shuffling feet across the carpet. There is apparently nothing that ties a specific spirit to the building. It is possible that just as troubled individuals seek comfort inside a church in life, the spirit of this lost boy may be seeking shelter in the most comforting place he could find.

Holloway Street

Closer to town there is a two-story brick house on Holloway Street that has had its share of unexplained events. The house stands on a hill above other houses in the area, and its architecture makes it look almost out of place. Originally built for and owned by an older couple, the man died shortly after moving into the house and left his widow to live there alone. She lived there for many years until her death, when the house was passed to a relative, who rented the property out. Many different people rented the house over the years, but not all of them experienced problems. It has been noted that only unmarried couples who live in the house experience activity.

One such couple had several unexplainable occurrences. The woman had a teenage son who took the room upstairs as his bedroom, while the woman and her boyfriend stayed in the master bedroom downstairs. Shortly after they moved in, the man and woman were sleeping when they were awakened by the sound of someone walking around in the room upstairs. The sound persisted throughout the night, and in the morning the mother asked the son why he had been up all night. He said that he had slept through the night and didn't know what she was talking about. She assumed that he was just sleepwalking. The sounds happened frequently, but it always was assumed that the son was sleepwalking or getting up in the night to use the bathroom—until one night when the young man slept over at a friend's house. The couple settled in to sleep and just as they began to doze, the sounds began again. The man, thinking that someone had broken into the house, got up and slowly crept up the stairs to investigate. The woman listened to his steps going up the stairs and to the continued sound of walking above her. As he reached the landing at the top of the stairs and opened the door slowly, she heard the walking stop. Upstairs, the man looked around and turned on the lights.

He cautiously searched the entire upper level of the house but found nothing. The walking sounds continued on through the years, along with other strange things, like feelings of dread when they were alone and objects going missing for days only to be found where they were before they were lost. One night, the couple went out of town, and the young man had some of his friends stay over. When the couple returned in the morning, they found one boy asleep on the floor in the living room. The woman woke him up and asked why he wasn't upstairs with the rest of the guys. The boy rubbed his eyes and explained that after they had all gone to sleep, he had awakened to go to the bathroom. As he got up to go to the bathroom, he came face to face with a haggard-looking old woman. Too frightened to scream, he staggered backward and fled down the stairs to the living room, where he was eventually able to fall asleep. He was so frightened that he vowed never to go upstairs again, and although he was the son's best friend, he never again returned to the second floor of the house. Even when the couple moved out a few years later, and the boy was helping them carry boxes, he stood at the bottom of the stairs and waited for someone to bring him boxes to take to the moving truck. After the couple married, all of the strange things that they had all become accustomed to ceased to happen. They spent several more uneventful years in the house, until they decided it was time to upgrade to a place of their own, and they bought a house.

The woman's son remained in the house on Holloway Street, along with his girlfriend, who moved in shortly after his mother and new husband left. Things seemed to be very peaceful for the first few weeks that the son and his girlfriend lived in the house together, and he didn't feel the need to tell her the story of the previous occurrences. With the help of his cousin, the young couple began to paint and make minor remodeling changes to the house to make it seem more like their own. The young man was working as a night security guard, so they would work during the day, and then he would leave his girlfriend alone in the house while he worked at night.

Late one night, he received a frantic call from his girlfriend. He could barely make out what she was saying, but he knew something was wrong. He called his cousin who had been helping him with the house to come and get him. The two men quickly went to the house and found the girlfriend sitting on the front stoop, sobbing and shaking. She had been sitting in the living room, watching television, when she suddenly heard a loud bang, followed by many small bangs and clatters. Surprised more than frightened, she ran to the dining room, where the disturbance had came from, and stopped in her tracks when she reached the room and saw what had caused the noise. The heavy wooden awning that was around the window in the room had been lifted from the wall and was across the room, as if it had been thrown across the table. The painting supplies that had been on the table were scattered across the room on the floor. Suddenly, the room turned cold, and she felt that she was no longer alone. She grabbed the phone and fled the house, leaving behind their pet potbellied pig.

When the two men entered the house, they found things just as she had described. They picked everything up and cleaned the room the best that they could. The awning had been torn from the nails on the wall, which had been holding it up, and it was all the way across the room. The pig was nowhere to be found, and a feeling of being watched was strong as the two men worked. When they finished, they went to the bathroom to wash up. As they were discussing what could have possibly happened, one of the men noticed a smudge on the mirror as the hot water created steam that rose out of the sink. He leaned forward and breathed on the mirror to expose the word "BYE" written on the glass of the mirror. They stopped and looked at each other and, without a word, fled the house, with the missing pig close behind. Soon after this happened, the couple was cleaning up after dinner in the kitchen. They were at the sink, washing dishes, when they heard a noise behind them and then a sound as if something hit the floor. They turned around to see that on the floor across the room were salt and pepper shakers that had belonged to the old woman and had been in the house since she and her husband had lived there. The couple figured that this was a final gesture from the house's previous owner and that she did not appreciate their living "in sin"—and she especially took offense at the use of her condiments.

They left the house shortly afterward and rented another place. Other couples have experienced similar situations, even down to the detail of the word "BYE" appearing in the mirror for other residents of the house. All of the couples who have reported these occurrences have been unmarried couples. Is the widow punishing the couples for living together unwed? Maybe the loss of her beloved husband left her bitter toward couples whom she does not feel worthy of sharing the same house as she shared with her husband.

Stagville Plantation

In beautiful northern Durham, near the community of Treyburn, is the sprawling Stagville Plantation. This North Carolina historical site is not only the largest plantation in North Carolina, but it also is one of the largest plantations in the South. Stagville is a more accurate example of the real working plantations that existed in the South during the antebellum period. Some of the plantations of this period that immediately come to mind would be some of the grand plantations of New Orleans that bring to mind scenes from *Gone With the Wind*. Most plantations, however, were more like the house and grounds of Stagville. The plantation house is plain compared to other southern plantations and is located amid a massive amount of agriculture. The Bennehan and Cameron families were wealthy landowners in the area, and by 1860, they had amassed an incredible amount of wealth, which included over three thousand acres and nine hundred slaves. Much of Durham today exists because of the wealth that families like the Bennehans and Dukes brought to the area. The site is spread out across several acres in northern Durham, and over the years it has had many reported sightings of a ghostly presence. On the Horton side of the plantation there stand several slave cabins, which the slaves built themselves. The structures are extremely impressive, as the slaves who constructed them had no training in carpentry, yet somehow the cabins still stand today as a testament to the resilience of a strong-willed people in trying times.

The slave quarters have been one of the hot spots of activity at Stagville. At these cabins, on more than one occasion, visitors have

Stagville Plantation in Durham.

reported seeing a small black girl standing by the houses and running and hiding from pursuers. People who see this little girl do not at first identify her as a spirit, and they often become extremely worried that she has been separated from her family. People have been concerned, even to the point of the police being called to file a report for a lost child. When the police arrive, the little girl or her family are never located, nor are there ever any reports from parents that their child is missing. Law enforcement officers have also been called out to respond to fires. The slave houses are part of the site at which there have been many reports of fire. Passersby have seen flames reaching for the sky from the doors and windows of the house. Many neighbors of the site also have called the fire department after seeing the flames. When the fire department arrives, there is never any trace of fire.

Across the street is the main house; here, there also have been reports of a great deal of activity that is unexplainable. Nightly the workers

Horton Grove of Stagville Plantation.

of the site lock up the building and set the alarm. Many times, they have left things in one room of the house, only to find the items in another room upon returning in the morning. Someone has moved the items without tripping the motion-detecting alarm system in the house. On the other hand, there are many instances of the motion detectors setting of the alarm from inside the house, yet no one is there when the authorities arrive, nor is there any sign of anyone breaking in or out. Employees feel cold spots and chills in certain parts of the house, even during the hot summer months. There are generally feelings of being watched by people who are alone in the house, and footsteps are heard around every corner.

The most interesting part about the spirits that call Stagville their home is the duality of the cultures that came together here. The ghosts around the slave cabins seem to draw attention to them. Are they trying to get people to look at them and truly understand what their struggle was? In the big house, the ghosts are more mischievous and seem to not want the attention; they just cause a little trouble. Are these spirits of the former residents or of the servants who labored there?

The Phantom Hitchhiker

Located along the rolling hills of northern Durham County and southwestern Granville County, there lies an area that once was a farming community known as Knapp of Reeds. Many families once called this area home until the outbreak of the Second World War called for the building of bases around the country to house and train soldiers headed for the battlefields in Europe, Africa and Asia. In 1942, families who had inhabited the area for almost two centuries were forced to pack up and leave the only home they had ever known to make way for Camp Butner, a United States Army combat infantry facility. Comprising sixty-three square miles, the camp included parts of Durham, Granville and Person Counties, which encompassed the entire Knapp of Reeds community. After the war, although the majority of the land was returned to the previous owners, many who had already started a new life elsewhere chose not return.

Though many did not return, they held close the stories and traditions of their former community and passed the history and the stories down from generation to generation. One such story involved a young man, a local farmer that had hired himself out for labor to another farm, and his experience with a strange, unseen hitchhiker.

The event, which happened around the turn of the twentieth century, left a deep impression on the young man named Paul. Paul, just like many of the local farmers, was poor. His family owned a small tract of land, and it took everyone pitching in to make ends meet in those days. When the opportunity arose to hire himself out as labor to another farm for a couple of weeks, he jumped at the chance to bring in some hard cash to

Knapp of Reeds, where a ghostly hitchhiker would catch a ride nightly with a local farmer.

help out at home and maybe pocket a little for himself. The work was hard; it required Paul to be at work early every morning before daylight, and the days wouldn't end until the blazing orange sun was setting in the sky, casting dark shadows along the rolling hills and valleys.

As it would be for the next two weeks, the night was extremely dark as a weary Paul hoisted himself up in the wagon seat for the several-mile journey back to their farm. On this first night as he left, he sat back as the horses walked down the old dirt road heading for home. Nearing a particular creek ford along the route, he felt the weight as if someone or something had hopped on the back of the wagon; at the same moment the horses became jittery and started acting strange, as if they were not happy with this unseen rider. Turning to see if he could catch a glimpse of who or what was now with him, he called out "hello," but there was no answer; "hello, who's there?" and still no answer. Paul could not even see his hand in front of his face much less whatever was sitting on the back of the wagon. He had no choice but to continue on, hoping that whatever was with him meant him no harm. After traveling about a mile, just as quickly as it hopped on, it hopped off, much to the relief of Paul and the agitated horses. It was a weary Paul who turned into home that night. He unhitched and fed the horses; once inside the house, the young man collapsed on the bed, too tired to eat.

The next day came early, and once again Paul set out for work. After hours off hard labor, he found himself once again on the road home. As the day before, the sun had gone down and the inky blackness enveloped him as he rode along in the pitch dark. Soon he was at the old creek ford, and just as it had the previous night at the same spot, the wagon was once more weighted down with an unseen rider. The horses became startled and the repeat of events caused the hairs on the back of Paul's neck to stand up. Again mustering up the courage to call out to this mysterious hitchhiker, he was met with only silence as he strained his eyes to look into the darkness. Just as before, about a mile down the road, the rider jumped off in exactly the same spot as the night before, leaving the man and his horses to proceed unmolested to their final destination. For the next two weeks, the same pattern continued. Every night, the rider would get on at the same spot and hop off at the same point—night after night and never seen by Paul.

At the end of the two weeks it was a relieved young man who received his pay. He made sure he left early that day to enjoy a peaceful ride home in the afternoon light. He never offered up an explanation as to the identity of the mysterious hitchhiker; he just passed the story down to his friends and family members until he passed away, allowing them to come to their own conclusions as to who or what this unseen rider was.

The area today is inhabited by some of those whose families decided to return with the leaving of the army and with some newcomers, most of whom have no idea of the history and the old stories of the area. Many of the old roads are either paved and are modern thoroughfares or are grown over and forgotten; only some are left who still remember traveling on them. Now, more than likely, a blacktop crosses over the old ford where, a century ago, a young man encountered a strange and unseen hitchhiker that he never forgot.

Pettigrew Street

A small mill house on Pettigrew Street in Durham served as a home for a poor working-class family whose father worked second shift at the cotton mill. One summer, the mother had to have gallbladder surgery. This left the oldest daughter, who was in her early teens, to take care of her younger brother and sister. The first night was a struggle; she fed them dinner and put them to bed after much fussing and fighting. She sighed as she finished tucking in her little sister and realized that she had a newfound respect for her mother and what she did on a daily basis. The young girl walked into the kitchen and took a glass from the cabinet. She filled the glass with ice and tap water as she looked around at the mess that the kids had made. How did Mom handle it every day? As she raised the glass to her lips, she heard a knock at the door. Who could it be at that time of night? She set the glass down and walked into the living room, feeling nervous that she was alone in the house with her brother and sister.

Many scenarios ran through her mind as she walked toward the front door. Maybe her mother had gotten worse at the hospital, or maybe her father had had an accident at the mill. When she reached the door, she peered through the curtain with caution and turned on the front porch light. No one was there. She wondered if maybe someone was playing a prank on her, and she opened the door to look around. Still no one was in sight. She closed the door, turned the light out and returned to the kitchen. As she reached the sink and started to clean up the dirty dishes, she realized that something was missing: her glass of water was gone. She looked around the kitchen but didn't see it. A strange feeling overtook her, and she walked over to the cabinet from which she had removed the glass. When she opened the door, she saw the glass sitting in the cabinet, bone dry, as if she had never taken it out. The girl was so shaken that she went straight to bed without cleaning the mess in the kitchen.

The next morning, she told her father what had happened, and he asked his in-laws if they could spend the night there so that his daughter wouldn't be scared. As the sun went down that night, they put the kids to bed and cleaned up after dinner. The children's grandparents were sitting in the living room, talking, when all of the sudden the grandfather went silent and stared down the hall. The grandmother looked at his face and asked what was wrong. He didn't answer. She stood up and looked down the hall to see her little grandson standing in the hall, white as a ghost. His eyes met hers and he said, "Did you see him? Did you see him?"

"See who?" she asked.

"The man—the old man with the beard," the boy said.

She assured him that there was no one there, and she walked him around to prove it to him. All the while, the grandfather sat silently in his chair, pretending to read the newspaper. When she calmed the boy and got him back to sleep, she returned to the living room and took her seat next to her husband. "What is going on around here lately?" she asked. "These kids are going crazy."

Her husband turned to her slowly and said, "He's not crazy. I saw him, too." He explained that as they were talking, he looked up to see their grandson coming out of his room and down the hall. Then he stopped dead in his tracks and looked over at the door to his sister's room. The grandfather followed the boy's gaze, and out of the door stepped an old man with a beard. He walked to the middle of the hall, in between him and his grandson. He could see right through him. Then the old man turned and looked straight at the grandfather. When he did this, he lowered his head, stepped back into the wall and disappeared. Strangely, after the mother returned from the hospital, nothing else was ever reported at the house—no strange feelings, knocks at the door or apparitions. Why did these things happen only during this short period of time? Maybe the spirit was only making its presence known to fill the void left in the house while the parents were away. Whatever it was it never came again or made itself known. The house no longer stands; it has become a victim of progress, as have many of the small mill houses on the streets in Durham, near where the old Erwin Mill used to stand.

Erwin Cotton Mill

Erwin Cotton Mills and Trinity College, which would later become Duke University, came to West Durham at the same time in 1892. By 1893, the mills were up and running and surrounded by mill houses that supported about 375 families. The mills had 11,000 spindles and 360 looms, which had helped to shift the textile industry from the North to the Southeast. One of the major reasons for this shift had been the cheap labor that was available in the South. The millworkers were like a close-knit family. They lived in mill houses and shopped in the same stores. They belonged to the same union, and many went to the same churches and schools. The textile boom only lasted about a century, and by the 1980s, mills began to shut down as technology and the expansion of outsourcing to other countries increased. By 1986, the West Durham Erwin Cotton Mills suffered the same fate and closed its doors forever. Hundreds of families had to start over, and West Durham began to decline until area revitalization a decade later. Although the mills no longer stand, many people still recall the sense of community and other memories from the days and nights spent working alongside friends and neighbors.

One day, near the end of the life of the mills, an old man who had worked there his whole life, just as his father had before him, began his day just as he always had. That day was different, though. He was drawing close to retirement, and he was trying to savor the sights and smells that he knew he would miss. On this day, he was going to change out the light bulbs in one of the weave rooms, and he grabbed his ladder and a box of bulbs and proceeded to make his way there. On the way, he talked to everyone. Stopping for a minute here and there, he soaked in the congratulations on his upcoming retirement from his coworkers and appreciated the fact that they all said how much they would miss having him around. He was a veteran of the mill, and everyone gave him respect and looked up to him.

He came to the weave room and found the regular faces that he would usually see there, except for a young maintenance worker who was working on one of the looms. The young man had not been there long, but the old man liked him. His father had worked at the mill for years, and the old man always had liked him, too. He took a moment to talk to the young man to see how things were going. They talked for a few moments before they got back to work, and the old man set up his ladder and climbed up to change the bulbs. The lights were high, and he remembered a time, years ago, when he had been terrified of heights, but a man does what he has to do to feed his family.

As he worked on the lights, he began to feel dizzy. He held on to the ladder tightly, but it was no use, and he fainted. He slumped and fell, sliding down the ladder, then away from it, down to the cold, hard concrete floor of the weave room. The young maintenance man who had just spoken to the old man watched him as he fell. His leg caught a rung in the ladder and made a grotesque snapping noise moments before his head struck the floor with a thud. Blood poured from his head, and as his co-workers tried to help him, they realized it was too late—he was already dead. He never made it to his long-deserved retirement from the mill.

Months later, the young man who had been working in the weave room when the old man had died was scheduled to open a wing of the mill one early morning. It was still dark outside when he came to the door of the building. There were very few other people at the mill at that time in the morning, and he felt alone and scared. He had tried to stay out of this wing ever since the accident, not because he was scared or superstitious, but it just brought back the vision of the old man hitting the ground. The sound of his impact made the young man's skin crawl. He turned the key and opened the door slowly to the large room lined with looms and pitch-black dark. He stepped inside, remembering that he had to walk down the center of the room to the other side to reach the breaker box that turned on the lights. As he began to walk across the room, he felt increasingly more alone and nervous. Under his breath, he whispered, "Damn, I wish the lights were on."

As he muttered these words, the lights came on with a snap. He stopped dead in his tracks and looked across the room to the breaker box. No one was there, and he was still alone. He finished his walk across the room and found that the breaker had been switched to the on position. He suddenly didn't feel alone anymore. He went about his business and continued to work, not telling anybody about his experience, for fear of being made to feel crazy. It was not until he was years removed from the mills that he was able to talk about what had happened. With time, he realized that whatever had turned the lights on for him that morning had not been trying to scare him but had simply been trying to help a neighbor.

Duke Hospital

The Duke family of Durham, North Carolina, made their fortune in the textile and tobacco industry and helped bring the city into the modern age, transforming Durham from a crossroads railroad town into a thriving business center in North Carolina's piedmont region. In 1924, James Buchanan Duke, who was living his final year, gave $40 million to create the Duke Endowment. His instructions included using $6 million to turn Trinity College into Duke University. When Duke died the next year, he left more money to the endowment, including $4 million to establish a medical school, a hospital and housing for nurses. As Duke lived out the last few years of his life, he envisioned bringing modern medicine to the Carolinas. James Duke's dream came true, and in 1930, Duke University Medical School was open, and by 1934, the school ranked among the top twenty medical schools in the nation. Today, Duke is consistently ranked amongst the top ten hospitals and medical schools in the nation.

Before the hospital was renovated, there were many reports of strange activities in the halls. One former Duke University police officer, who worked in the hospital, has recollections of more than one eerie experience there. He claims that on many occasions, the elevator would open with a ding while nobody was around. The elevator doors would stay open for a moment and then close while the elevator stayed stationary. One night, as he walked along the empty halls, the elevator opened as he passed it. Curiosity overtook him, and he stepped into the empty elevator. He looked around at the walls and the buttons, and then he heard the doors close behind him. He turned to hit the "Open" button, as he now felt uneasy, but the elevator started with a jolt. The elevator stopped on the third floor, and the doors opened. There was no one in sight. He walked down the hall to the nurses' station and asked the young nurse at the desk if anyone had called the elevator up. She said that they had not. She had been the only one on the hall for hours. Although he found it strange, the officer refused to believe that anything ghostly had taken place.

On another occasion, the officer was asked to escort a nurse to a desolate part of the hospital to retrieve some supplies. As they walked down the hall, the nurse talked endlessly of the many "ghost stories" she had heard over the years and how she appreciated his walking with her. As they reached the supply room, he opened the door and propped it with a wedge at the bottom. He stood in the doorway and waited while the nurse pulled bandages and other supplies off the shelves. With his arms folded, he watched her take down what she needed, and she thanked him once again for coming with her.

"I don't know what you guys are so scared of," he said. "There's no ghost here."

Almost instantaneously, he was struck from behind by the door, which knocked him almost to his knees. Sure that someone had pushed against the door, he turned quickly and pushed the door open. The hall was empty, as it had been before. On the floor in the hall was the wooden wedge that he had used to prop the door open. There was no sign of anyone who could have slammed the door, and he felt uneasy on his way back down the hall. He never experienced any other ghostly encounters, but he was often told of situations that other members of the staff experienced. He remained skeptical, but he never found courage to refute anyone's story in the hospital again.

The Haunted Wood

Located in eastern Durham County there is a large tract of woods that are now part of the Butner Falls of Neuse state lands. The lands include recreational areas, hiking trails, parks and game lands for hunting and fishing. When the state took the property for the area in the 1970s, many of the local residents were forced to move from the homes and land that their families had inhabited for years, although it appears that some restless family members may have been left behind.

During the tumultuous days of Prohibition, the coves and hollers, with their beautiful flowing creeks, were known to hide the stills of several local moonshiners. Even in the recent past one could see evidence of this illegal production when straying off of the beaten path. Several of the old homeplaces exist that were involved in the selling of the liquor; most are now just decaying remnants of days gone by. Around these old homesteads is where much of the activity is reported. Many who have been caught in these woods after dark have reported seeing strange lights move from the site of one of the old homes in particular to the bottoms around the creeks. The lights are described as a yellowish glow moving very slowly down an old path where it disappears once it reaches an old ford in the stream. Could this be one of the old moonshiners slipping out to check his still or just the reflection from a flashlight of someone moving through the woods? If it is the reflection of a flashlight, why does it always follow the same old path and disappear not to be seen again, and why is no rustling or movement heard in the leaves? The appearances have left many baffled for those very same reasons.

Another strange occurrence around the same area is that of a little girl who calls out to those in the area. This usually occurs from about dusk to early nighttime. Strangely, several of the reports of those who have heard her said that she called them by name. Of course, once they hear the voice of a little girl call their name, they immediately search the area for someone they believe to be in trouble. Upon completion of the search, they realize that they have been alone the whole time, and they

The haunted woods in Durham, where many have seen ghostly lights and heard the voice of a little girl.

begin to wonder how she knew their name. This usually sends the person scurrying to make a hasty retreat to their vehicle.

Another story involving what is believed to be the same little girl was told by an elderly widow who resided close to the area where the voices have been heard. It was early one evening when the woman had decided to go to bed. She went through her normal routine getting ready, turned out the lights, looked outside and then locked up the house. Once in her bedroom, she had no sooner laid her head on the pillow when she heard what sounded like a little girl singing and talking to herself. Concerned, she got up and looked out her bedroom window but was unable to see anything. Believing that she had just been hearing things, she once again lay back down to go to sleep. She had lain there only a moment when once again she heard the loud giggle of a small girl. Getting up, she looked out of the bedroom window once again and saw nothing. Just then, a frightful thought came to her: what if one of her small great-granddaughters who lived nearby had come outside and was playing outside of her home? Immediately, she called her grandson on the phone and told him what was going on; he set her fears to rest when he told her that the granddaughters were safe inside the house, but that still did not explain the singing and laughter of the little girl. The grandson told her he would walk down to her house and have a look.

Once he arrived, he conducted a thorough search of the area and was unable to locate anything. The grandmother was distraught; she knew that she had heard the voice of a little girl, and she was sure that there was a small child lost in those woods. That's when the grandson reluctantly told the grandmother that years before, when he was no more than ten years old, he too had heard the voice of a little girl. He had been in her front yard looking through a telescope just as it had become dark when the voice of a little girl called his name from the woods. Not sure he had heard correctly, he looked up from his telescope and once again heard very clearly a little girl call out his name once again. Frightened, he dragged his telescope behind him as he ran all the way up the old dirt road to his house. He told his grandmother that he had never told anyone, because after it was all over, he had began to doubt himself and what he had heard. Interestingly enough, the grandmother's bedroom window faced the same section of woods where the reports of the little girl's voice has always originated. The grandmother never heard the little girl again, or she never spoke of her again. Who is this little girl who calls out to others and giggles and plays in the early evening darkness? Was she a little girl lost or one just cut short in this life and looking for a playmate in the afterlife? We will probably never know her true identity; we can only hope that she can find the peace of whomever, or whatever, she is looking for.

If one is walking through the area, it is still advisable to stay on trails and the open areas, for the woods even today can give an individual a confused sense of direction. Even with its proximity to the cities, it is very easy to get turned around and lost, and many of the areas in the park are very secluded, possibly increasing the wary hiker's chance of bumping into one of these visions of the past.

PART III

RALEIGH

After the American Revolution, the colonial capital of North Carolina in New Bern was abandoned as the meeting site for the General Assembly, which in turn gathered at different locations around the state. In 1788, it was decided by the General Assembly that a new capital for North Carolina should be built in Wake County on one thousand acres that had been purchased by Joel Lane. The new city would be named Raleigh, in honor of Sir Walter Raleigh. By 1792, Raleigh was officially established as the Wake County seat and the state capital. The General Assembly met there for the first time in 1794, and in 1796, the new state capital building was finished. The original two-story brick building was later expanded to meet the growing needs of the government.

Raleigh is located near the center of the state of North Carolina, and it also has the distinction of being one of only a few cities in the United States that was founded and laid out as a capital city. The origins of the settlement that predated the city of Raleigh date back to the formation of Wake County, which was named after Margaret Wake, the wife of colonial governor William Tryon. In 1858, Peace College for Women was established in Raleigh, making it the first of many institutions of higher learning to come to the capital city. Peace was followed by Meredith College, which was another women's college, in 1891.

The skyline of Raleigh.

Raleigh

After the Civil War and the emancipation of the slaves, Raleigh became a gathering place for freedmen from around the state and the rest of the South. Shaw University held classes in Raleigh as early as 1865, making Shaw the first historically black college in the South. Also, Shaw University's Leonard Medical Center was the first four-year medical school in the state, as well as in the South. St. Augustine College followed Shaw in 1867 and has helped to cement a large middle-class African American population in the city, which would not become common in many other Southern cities until much later.

Raleigh is also home to North Carolina State University, which was founded in 1887 as a land grant college. North Carolina State has traditionally served as a hub for the agriculture and textile industries in the state. The Wolf Pack of North Carolina State rounds out the "big three" of collegiate sports in the state, along with the Blue Devils of Duke University in Durham and the Tar Heels of the University of North Carolina. The epic battles of these three schools have made the Triangle one of the hottest spots for college sports. Even transplants to the area will find that they have to make a choice between one of these schools or be left on the sidelines during Monday morning quarterback sessions.

After being spared by General Sherman during the Civil War, Raleigh has continued to move forward as one of the leading cities in North Carolina, as well as in the South. Like many Southern cities, Reconstruction stymied growth for many years, but Raleigh was one of the first cities to rebound and continue to grow as it had prior to the war. The reasons behind Raleigh's success through hard times can be found in the eclectic and diverse nature of its makeup. From the colleges and universities to the population itself, Raleigh has always been a place for anyone—and a place where change was welcomed.

Today, aside from being home to a beautiful Victorian governor's mansion, majestic oak-lined streets and Mordecai Square—which includes the birthplace of the seventeenth president of the United States, Andrew Johnson—Raleigh has progressed with the times, becoming a center of modern industry. Raleigh also is home to institutions of research, government and higher learning. Raleigh is an excellent example of a city that has developed into a progressive metropolitan area, while still preserving the heritage and traditions of its past.

Mordecai Historical Park

Some of the most famous haunts in North Carolina reside in one place, the Mordecai Historical Park in Raleigh. The park is centered on Mordecai Manor and includes the birthplace of Andrew Johnson, a kitchen, a garden and replicas of a post office from 1847, a law office from 1810 and a small church from 1840. The state purchased the property from the Mordecai family in 1967 and moved these other historic buildings to this location over the following years. Mordecai Manor was built in 1785 by Joel Lane for his son Henry. Lane owned over five thousand acres in the area and grew many different crops, such as cotton, corn and wheat.

When city planners came together to plan the city of Raleigh about 1792, they first considered the land of Colonel John Hinton across the Neuse River, but before the final decision was made, Lane had some of the high-ranking members of the committee over for dinner and drinks. This tipped the balance in favor of Joel Lane, and the state purchased one thousand acres. Over the years, the Lanes' land served to help the growth of Raleigh and the surrounding area. When Joel Lane died, his son Henry took over the homestead. The name of the house originates from Moses Mordecai, who married Henry Lane's oldest daughter, Margaret. Moses had three children with Margaret before she died, and in a gesture of loyalty toward the Lane family, he married Margaret's younger sister, Ellen, and had a daughter that they named after his first wife. Moses Mordecai commissioned William Nichols to add on to the house, and he created the structure that stands today. Mordecai passed the house on to his children, and eventually his youngest daughter, Margaret, took over as the mistress of the house. She and then her descendants owned the house until 1967, when it was put on the market. The state bought the property and turned it and the surrounding area into the historic park that exists today.

The Mordecai Mansion in Raleigh.

The house contains over 75 percent of the family's original belongings. One of these items is a piano that had been with the family for years. On many occasions during tours of the house, the guides and tour groups have heard music coming from the room with the piano, but when they reach the room, the music stops and no one is present in the room. One of the most famous stories of an encounter in the house is that of a housekeeper. She was cleaning up after everyone had gone when she saw one of the guides walking down the hall from the library. This was strange, as she was sure that she was alone in the house. As the lady drew near, she could see that she was dressed in a black pleated skirt and a white shirt with a black tie. The woman walked past the housekeeper as if she was not there and went into the parlor. Something just didn't seem right about the lady, so the housekeeper followed her into the parlor. As the staff member entered the parlor, she realized that her first impression had been correct. She was totally alone in the house. Shaken up, she continued to work, but she couldn't get rid of the feeling of familiarity of the woman that she had just encountered. As she was finishing up to go, she noticed a picture on the wall, one that she had seen a thousand times but never paid a lot of attention to—it was a portrait of the lady of the house herself, Margaret Mordecai, the woman she had seen enter the parlor.

Another building on the property that holds a mysterious presence is the birthplace of Andrew Johnson. The small wooden house was moved to the historical park shortly after the state bought the property, and there have been several reports by staff members and guests of candlelight in the building at night, when no one is on the property. Also, many who have worked there or have visited the building claim to feel a sense of dread and foreboding in the house. Many describe the feeling of not being alone or of being watched by an unseen entity. Could Andrew Johnson have returned to the place of his birth and his innocence? Johnson was the chief executer of the nation during a very trying time in our nation's history. He was born in Raleigh in 1808 to Jacob and Mary, who worked

Raleigh is the birthplace of seventeenth president Andrew Johnson.

Lights can often be seen in the upper window of the Andrew Johnson House.

for Casso's Inn. Mary was a weaver, and Jacob was a hostler and part-time janitor at the state capital. Andrew Johnson came from extremely humble beginnings and never received any formal education. He taught himself to read and write, and when his father died after trying to save two friends from drowning, Andrew was apprenticed out to a tailor to help support his family. He was truly the only president who was a self-made man. After the assassination of President Lincoln, Johnson served as the commander in chief during the Reconstruction era, one of the most trying and stressful times over which any president has presided. Could the stress and pressure of the presidency have driven his spirit back to the place of his beginnings?

North Carolina State Capitol

After the end of the Revolutionary War, many state government buildings were erected throughout the newly formed country. In North Carolina, a small building was erected in 1796 and was upgraded in 1822. In 1831, a worker doing some construction on the capitol building accidentally burned the structure down. In 1832, the state General Assembly approved $50,000 for the construction of a new capitol building and announced its construction on July 4, 1833. They decided that they would spare no expense on the new building and that it would be an example for other states in the Union. The state hired Ithiel Townsend Alexander and Jackson, a firm from New York, to do the job. The architecture company had just completed the capitol in New Haven, Connecticut, and was working on the state capitol in Indianapolis, Indiana. The final cost for the capitol building was $533,000, and it still stands out today as one of best-preserved examples of Greek Revival architecture in the South. Some state capitols are bigger or more ornate in their design, but none are more closely associated with the time in which they were built than the North Carolina state capitol. The building appears just as it did upon completion, in many cases down to the furniture in the offices and halls. With time, the building became too small for the various offices to function there, so in 1888 the State Supreme Court and the State Library moved out. Then, in 1963, the General Assembly moved into the newly built legislature building.

Today, only the governor and lieutenant governor remain at the capitol building—or so many think. One longtime night watchman, who has since retired, has told of many encounters with the unexplained in the large, empty halls of the capitol. He has told of walking down the halls in the dead of night and hearing footsteps behind him. When he turned around, no one was ever there. Also, on many occasions he would secure a door and proceed down the hall to the next one, when suddenly he would hear the door he just passed slam shut. When this first began to happen, he would immediately rush back to the door to see who had opened it. Maybe someone had been hiding inside and

North Carolina's state capitol building in Raleigh.

fled when he passed the door. Always, when he got back to the door, he found no one there, only the empty halls and rooms. In the library, on some quiet nights, he heard books falling on the floor, but as he scanned the room, none was ever found. Many times over he years he heard a violent breaking of glass near him. He rushed toward the sound of the damage, but in all of his years, he never found any broken windows. Quick glances of shadows, voices around corners and elevators moving in the middle of the night by themselves became normal occurrences to the night watchman. The most eerie of all of the accounts from the late-night visits were the accounts of faint gospel music played in the distance down the long halls.

The encounters have not been limited to the night watchman. Many of the employees of the state capitol building have reported being touched by icy cold hands, as well as hearing books fall in the library during the daylight hours when no one is present. An apparition has even been seen wandering the halls of the old building late in the evening, after the majority of the employees have left.

Executive Mansion

In 1883, then governor of North Carolina Thomas Jarvis authorized the building of the current executive residence that stands now at Burke Square. The house was completed in 1891 and still stands today as a crown jewel in the capital city. The construction of the mansion was a tedious project that was taxing on the state's budget. Prisoner labor was used in the building of the house, and inscriptions from the prisoners can still be seen there today. The first governor to occupy the mansion was Daniel Fowle, who moved into the mansion before it was actually finished but wanted to gain public support for its completion. Unfortunately for Governor Fowle, he did not occupy the house for long—at least not in the realm of the living. He and his son moved in on January 5, 1891— his wife having died some years earlier—but Governor Fowle died three months later on April 7, 1891. Though his time in the house was brief, he made many personal touches to the house. One of his additions was the bed that he had especially made for the mansion. The bed was extra wide to accommodate the governor and his young son, who sometimes slept with him and was prone to tossing and turning. The governor was actually found dead in this bed by his son, after having died in his sleep.

The room where the governor died became known as the Governor Fowle Room. All successive governors used the bedroom and bed until 1969, when Bob Scott was elected and moved into the house. Governor Scott tried to sleep in the bed, but it was far too short for his large frame, and it creaked with age as he tried to sleep at night. He soon brought in a modern bed and moved Fowle's bed to the third floor. Soon after he made this move, he and his wife began to experience what they believe was the late governor's protest. They were in bed about 10:00 p.m. when they

The Executive Mansion in Raleigh may be the home of more than one governor at a time.

both heard a knocking sound that seemed to be coming from inside of the wall where the headboard of the old bed used to be. Governor Scott pressed his ear against the wall and listened as the knocking continued. The sound was extraordinarily similar to that of a ball dropping and bouncing on the ground. The first knock was loud and was followed a few seconds later by the next knock. The knocks became closer and closer together, finally coming back to back in quick succession before stopping. The next morning, Scott searched for answers throughout the mansion. He questioned staff members and checked the plumbing and electrical systems throughout the house. There was no explanation for the sounds. The knocking occurred every night for the duration of the governor's term in the mansion. When he left office, the next governor soon brought Fowle's bed back down to the second floor and restored it to its former place in the house. Since the bed has been restored to the Governor Fowle Room, there have been no reports of activity in the house.

Poole Road Ghost

Along the area that is today known as Poole Road in Raleigh, there was once a mighty forest. The forest and the land were owned by William Poole, but since his death the area has been made into suburbs, parking lots and strip malls. William R. Poole was born on October 8, 1796, and soon turned his life into a profitable existence. It is rumored that he began his business career at a young age with fifty cents to his name. He turned this into one of the biggest spreads of land in North Carolina during the period leading up to the Civil War. Poole was a big man, and he used to ride a big white horse that was so majestic that all of the people would stop and stare at him as if he was royalty when he passed. He would spend entire days riding through his 1,600 acres of woods. He would study the trees, and he loved the trees so much that he rarely allowed any to be cut down.

William Poole's success continued, and his wealth grew up until the Civil War, when, like almost every other wealthy landowner in the South, he began to suffer the effects of the war. Near the end of the war, the Yankees moved toward Raleigh at a rapid pace. North Carolina had been relatively spared by Sherman for its initial reluctance to go to war, but the major problems came from the scoundrels and raiders who followed the army. William Poole met this threat one sunny day while sitting alone on his porch. He watched as the half-blue, half-brown soldiers rode down the long road leading to his house. He was alone, having lost all of his slaves at the news of the Union army's presence. The raiders had heard that Poole had hidden a small fortune somewhere on his property and had come to make him talk. He would have none of it, even after he was dragged behind a horse to his biggest mill and forced to watch it being burned to the ground. He was beaten badly, and as they set off through the woods, looking for his hiding place, a soft whinny was heard in a thick stand of oak trees. The raiders set off in the direction of the sound, and Poole finally broke and began to plead with the men to leave the horse alone. It was too late. The Yankees rode into the clearing and found Poole's most prized possession—his white stallion. He was tied to a tree with plenty of slack, and there had been hay and water left for him. It was the most beautiful horse they had ever seen. Poole had tried to hide the one possession that he could not replace, but because of the horse's loneliness, he had been discovered. Satisfied, they pushed Poole off the horse he was riding and left him laying in the dirt. He watched as the men rode away on his beloved horse.

After the war, Poole's success continued as he served as justice of County Court of Pleas and Quarter Sessions and chairman of the Board of County Commissioners. He even helped in the building of the courthouse in 1882. He died at the age of ninety-three, and in his will he decreed that the woods he had loved for so many years would be preserved around his grave. For many years, the woods went untouched, until eventually people began to move out from the city and slice into these hallowed woods. Soon after people began to traverse these woods, there circulated the stories of a rider on a large white horse. The rider was always just far enough away from the person to keep from being seen clearly. One thing was obvious, though: the rider was more than fit for the massive horse on which he rode. The horse and rider were truly a magnificent sight, but no one ever came close enough to see who it was. Other stories told of the sound at night of heavy footsteps around people's houses. Children sleeping would be awakened by the sound of walking outside their windows. The story goes that the father would go outside with his lantern or flashlight and would find incredibly large footprints leading to nowhere. All of the ghostly activity has, with time and progress, come to an end. Children play outside and sleep soundly at night in the houses along Poole Road today, but people still remember the days when children ran hard to beat the sun home, in hopes that the rider would not make an appearance.

North Carolina State University

North Carolina State University was founded as a state agricultural college. Near the campus, off of Hillsborough Street, is an eighteenth-century house that has been remodeled to accommodate college students with affordable housing. After their freshman year, a group of girls from State decided that they didn't want to live on campus the upcoming year, so they rented the house. At the end of the year, their families came and helped them move out of the dorm across campus into their new residence. The girls were looking forward to staying in Raleigh over the summer in their newfound freedom of unsupervised living. Soon after the girls moved in, they began to awaken at night to sounds of someone walking throughout the house. They would come together in fear and walk through the house, as the sounds of footsteps moved away from them. They never found anyone in the house. After a while, the sound became common and did not frighten them as much as it bothered them to know that something was there that they could not see.

One day after classes had started, one of the girls was preparing for class when she walked by the spare room that was used for exercising. She noticed the heavy bag that was hanging from the ceiling was swinging wildly. She thought that one of her roommates must have pushed it when she walked by. As she packed her books into her book bag, she realized that all her roommates had been gone for hours. She looked again at the hanging bag as it swayed back and forth, and she felt the hair on her neck rise. She hurriedly packed her bag and fled the house. As the school year passed, the girls became accustomed to their uninvited roommate's presence. When the girls had first moved into the house, they had noticed that the door to the bathroom would not latch shut. They could shut the door, but it could be pushed open from the outside. The girls were comfortable with this—having spent one year together in a dorm, they had waved goodbye to privacy long ago. Living in the house, though, they found that every time they went to the bathroom, the door would slowly open until it was opened all the way. All of the girls took this as a sign from the "ghost" that he was there, but they were never really convinced that it was not just the way the house was constructed or a joke from a roommate.

One weekend, all of the girls went home except for one, whose parents came to visit her for the weekend. While they were there, her father noticed the bathroom door. He took some time the next morning to go to the hardware store and get the needed materials to make the door shut. On Sunday evening, she stood on the front porch and waved goodbye to her parents as they drove off into the dusk. She turned and went back into the house to wait for her roommates, who would be home soon. While she waited, she decided she would take a bath. She went upstairs to draw the tub and light some candles. She closed and latched the door, pulling back on it to make sure it was closed and impressed by the handiness of her old man. She undressed and slid into the bath water, as relaxation once again set in. She loved her parents, but sometimes they could just be too much. She enjoyed her freedom and her life away from home and her family. As she reflected on these things, out of the corner of her eye she noticed something move. She turned and saw the door opening, as if someone was pushing on it. "Hello," she said, but there was no response. The doorknob slowly turned, and the door opened. "Hello," she said again, as she pulled her towel up around her and got out of the tub. The door continued to open slowly until it stood open all the way. No one was there. Terrified, she quickly dried off, dressed and left the house as rapidly as she could. No matter how many times the girls had the door fixed to the bathroom, it would never stay closed if they were inside. The occurrences persisted the entire time the girls lived in the house. As they stood in front of the house for the last time after graduation, they could not help but wonder if the next residents would have the same problems that they had had in the house. They never came back to find out.

Crybaby Lane

Off Western Boulevard near Pullen Park there is an open field that seems out of place. As you walk through the tall grass, it is apparent that a structure used to stand there. It is said that an orphanage used to be located there in that lonely field, one that housed young children and infants. One night, the orphanage caught fire, and as the fire blazed, the caretakers tried to rescue as many of the children as possible. As the priests and nuns who ran the orphanage stood outside of the burning building with the children who had escaped, they listened to the cries and screams of the babies who they could not save as they died in a most horrible manner. The smoke filled the night sky with gloom and sadness. When morning came, the local authorities went through the debris and took a toll of the carnage. It is said that dozens of babies and toddlers were trapped in the large house and died there.

Today, the rumor is that, in the evening, you can hear the cries of babies blowing on the wind across the field. Being at the end of a long side road, it has been the occurrence more than once that a young couple have parked there, seeking a private place to do what young couples tend to do. To make the mood a little more in his favor, the young man would likely tell the story to the young woman as he rolled the windows down. She would slide closer to him and hold him close, as the cries blew in through the windows and sealed the deal for the young man. Apparently, the legend is just that: a legend.

In fact, there was an orphanage where the field is today, and it did burn down. But the orphanage was not a facility that housed children of all ages. The orphanage was for young men who had no family and were training for the priesthood. The night the big house burned down there were no fatalities, although one boy broke his leg jumping from a second-story window to escape the flames. Crybaby Lane is a perfect example of how urban legends begin and evolve over the years. The moral of the story is that, although legends and ghost stories are fun, the truth is in the history.

The Lost Boy

The evening mist hung low over the leaf-littered road winding through the countryside. The early stages of fall had arrived, and the leaves of the hardwoods looked as if they were on fire. A young boy, who we will call Randy, was playing in the backyard of his home. As with most young boys who live out in the country, his mind wandered to the deep woods around his home, and inside was a deep burning desire to explore the unknown. The evening silence was broken when his mother, watching him from a back window, called out to him that she was bringing him a jacket to wear in the evening chill. Little did she know that as she called out to him that would be the last time she would see her son alive.

When she came out, Randy was nowhere to be found. The mother began to call his name, walking around the house and yard; realizing that he was missing, she frantically began to walk through the edge of the woods, screaming his name and pleading for him to please respond. Once notified, the Wake County Sheriff's Office responded, as did the entire community. Unlike today, thirty years ago that area of northern Wake County near present-day Falls Lake, with it's hiking trails and recreation areas, was a rural community, where everyone knew one another and all chipped in to help a neighbor in need. The locals turned out in droves and immediately ventured out in search parties, combing the local area.

A lot of prayers went up for that little boy, because all of the locals knew how cold and dark it could get in those woods and how frightened that child must have been. But after all of the praying and searching, every one's worst fears were realized when, after a while, the boy's cold, lifeless body was found leaning against a tree, it was if he had sat down to rest and just fell asleep. The community that had come together to search was now gathered together to mourn and lay little Randy to rest.

As time went on, the family moved away, leaving the little home empty and forlorn. Seasons came and went; spring rains turned into hot dry summers, which turned to brisk falls and cold winters. Every year, new layers of leaves were added to the remote site where little Randy spent his last hours on this earth…or were they truly his last?

In the mid-1990s, two local teenagers had spent the day fishing at Falls Lake. Both boys were enjoying themselves so much that time had slipped away from them, and before they knew it the sun was disappearing from the evening sky, casting strange shadows through the tops of the trees. Gathering their equipment, the boys headed for the old logging road that

Does the spirit of a lost little boy still walk these woods trying to find his way home?

led to the main highway. The feat proved much more difficult without the light of day to guide their steps. Try as they might, they could not locate the logging road in order to escape the inky blackness that now surrounded them. The two wandered around aimlessly for what seemed like hours, walking around in circles, sure that they were close to their destination. That is when they first heard it. At first, it started as a faint cry or whimper. Both boys looked at each other a little confused at first, but this quickly changed over to excitement once they realized that they had to be near civilization, a main road, a home or something, anything to get them out of those woods. They began to walk toward the sound of the crying; it became louder and louder the farther they went, but it always seemed to stay just ahead of them, just out of their reach. The boys were beginning to be a bit unnerved, but common sense told them that they were steadily making way toward some type of human contact.

Just as the boys were about to give up, they noticed that they no longer heard the pitiful crying sound any more. They stood there for a moment waiting to see if the sound returned, but it did not. As they stood there, baffled, a light began to slowly move through the trees; it was the headlights of a car. The boys made their way out of the woods. Recognizing the old back road they were on, they started the long journey back to their vehicle parked on the main highway.

Exhausted, the boys drove home and went straight to bed, too tired to think about the strange ordeal they had experienced that night. It wasn't until the next morning that one of the boys awoke and began to give serious thought to the unexplainable events of the previous night. Why was there no sign of anyone when they had come from the woods? If it had been a child crying, surely there had to be someone around when they made their exit, but yet there was no one. Sure that he had recognized the area where the boys exited the woods, the young man got dressed and took a drive to the old back road where crying sound had stopped. As soon as he pulled off the main highway onto the back road, an eerie feeling came over him. He was now sure that he knew where he was. The old homeplace was deserted and run down, covered over now with vines. That's the area where they had emerged from the woods the night before; he knew it now as the place at which, the old folks had told him, a little boy had once lived and had gotten lost and froze to death before he could be found. Now a grown man himself, he honestly believes that the spirit of the little boy led him and his friend out of the woods that night. Though grateful, he still to this day refuses to fish in that area.

Old Grocery Store

In the late nineties, a young man was working as an assistant manager for a local food chain, the chain's oldest location in Raleigh. He was working a closing shift from one o'clock in the afternoon until eleven o'clock at night. Prior to his arrival at the store, it had been a twenty-four-hour location, and the night manager, Steve, had not changed his schedule to accommodate the store closing. He would work in the store alone overnight and would be relieved in the morning at seven.

The assistant manager had concerns that Steve was not getting a lot done being in the store by himself. That night, he surprised Steve when he came in and said he was going to take a break and come back to work overnight with him to make sure he was productive. He took about a one-hour break and then came back to the store about midnight. The assistant manager let himself in, locked the door behind him and found Steve working moving some boxes in the back room. They worked together, moving things around and organizing boxes for several hours. About three o'clock in the morning, they were on the loading dock that looked into the back room when, suddenly, a man walked across the back room and through the doors leading to the meat department. He was not transparent and did not pass through the doors like they were not there. The doors swung open just as if a person had passed through them. The assistant manager yelled behind him because the store had been closed for several hours, and he was not sure if the man had been locked in the store or if he was there for malicious intents such as a robbery.

The manager followed behind him into the meat department, quickly yelling "sir," and then out onto the sales floor. He was gone. The manager looked all over the store and went to the front and checked the locks to make sure they had not been tampered with. They had not. Confused, he began to walk back to the loading dock to go back to what he was doing. On the way back, he began to wonder where Steve had been while he was chasing the elusive intruder, and he became angry at the fact that Steve had not given him any kind of backup whatsoever. He could have been getting brutally murdered, and where was Steve?

The manager came around the corner, and there Steve was in the same place he had left him. Steve had not moved, not one inch, during the manager's pursuit of the strange man in their store. He immediately lit into Steve. "Where in the hell were you when I needed you? I could be getting murdered right now, and you could care less."

Steve hardly changed his expression or looked up at the manager during his tirade. Then, finally, he spoke the few simple words that ended the manager's night and sent him walking rapidly out to his car. "I see him all the time."

The young man never worked overnight in that store again, and he was always ready to go when it came time to close the store. He never told anyone this story, not even his wife, until a few years later when he had been working at another store in Raleigh and got transferred back to the store where he saw the man. He was talking to another employee in the back aisle by the meat department when she looked past him and nodded as if to greet someone. Then her face changed to a look of distress. Her face lost its color and she became speechless.

The young man followed her glance down an empty aisle and asked her what was wrong. She told him that while they had been talking, a man walked from an aisle toward them. He had walked toward the meat department and made eye contact with her as she spoke with him. She smiled and nodded, thinking he was a customer that may have a question, but as he drew nearer, she said he just disappeared like he had never been there. She was obviously scared and confused at what had happened, and as she related her story to him, he began to think of what had happened to him so long ago. If he was crazy, then at least he knew that he was not alone in his insanity.

He no longer works at that location, but the store is still open. To this day, he occasionally hears from some of the store's current employees that there are still some things that happen that are out of the ordinary: strange sounds at night when no one is in the store with the employees, as well as shadows in the corner of people's eyes as they venture to the back room to set the alarm at night.

Dorothea Dix Hospital

Dorothea Dix was born in 1802 to a father that was a Methodist preacher, as well as an abusive alcoholic, and a mother who suffered from many ailments, including mental illness. After a tumultuous childhood, Dorothea dedicated her life to teaching and to caring for the mentally ill. At the time, the mentally ill were often put out of sight and out of mind in what were at the time referred to as lunatic asylums. Although her father was an abusive man, he did have a great influence on her life. He taught her to read and write at a young age, which put her well ahead of other girls her age who did not have the same educational opportunities as she had. At the age of fifteen, she opened her first school for girls and would continue to educate young ladies for the next twenty-four years.

When she was thirty-nine years old, she volunteered to teach a Sunday school class for female inmates at the East Cambridge Jail in Massachusetts. She was horrified at the conditions of the jail and found that all of the inmates were put together regardless of the situation. She found that the mentally ill and mentally challenged patients shared the same space with violent criminals and prostitutes. She took her complaints to the state legislature in Massachusetts and eventually won her case, leading to many drastic changes in the way the mentally ill were cared for in the state. When she won her victory in Massachusetts, she took her show on the road and began to tour other states and push for change.

In 1848, North Carolina and Delaware were the only remaining states of the thirteen original colonies that did not have a system in place to care for the mentally ill. Dorothea came to North Carolina that year and began to lobby for the creation of a hospital where these unfortunate citizens could be cared for properly. With the untiring help of Dorothea Dix, the hospital was built and served the state of North Carolina for over one hundred years.

Near the end of the hospital's service, but before the hospital closed down, there were many nights on which an entire floor would be empty. Although there were no patients on the floor, the hospital administration required that there be a nurse at the floor's information desk at all times. The ladies that manned the desk on the empty halls often found themselves surrounded by the sounds of former residents. Many reported the sound of wheels rolling down the empty halls and doors opening and closing on their own. Sometimes the dead silence of the night would be shattered by

The screams of patients from the past still resonate through the halls at Dorthea Dix Hospital.

a blood-curdling scream that resonated down the dark hallway and many times sent the nurse scurrying to the elevator and frantically pressing the down button.

Over the years, the hospital has needed much work to keep the facilities current and up to date. Many workers have helped in the maintenance and renovation to the facility. Several of the plumbers and electricians tell the same story of having to bring a radio with them while they worked because of the unearthly screams that sounded throughout the halls. The hospital no longer functions as an institution for the mentally ill and waits for the state to decide what its future holds, but the old empty building still houses the spirits of the patients who suffered for years—prisoners in their own bodies and now prisoners for eternity in the hospital's lonely halls.

White-Holman House

Hidden from the street near the state capitol and the executive mansion stands a two-story white house that serves as an office. Just looking at the house gives no indication of the historical significance it holds for Raleigh. The house is one of the oldest standing structures in the capital city and has housed some of the most important people in the history of North Carolina. The house was built by William White some time between 1798 and 1810, while he served as secretary of state for North Carolina. William White had four daughters: Emma, Susan, Sophronia and Eleanor. The fact that William White served North Carolina as secretary of state was not the family's only claim to history. Eleanor was married to David L. Swain, who was the governor of North Carolina in the 1830s and served as the president of the University of Chapel Hill during the tumultuous days of Reconstruction.

The White family held the house until 1884, when it was sold to William Calvin Holman for $2,422.25. Holman was a transplant from Massachusetts, who had married Miss Anna Belo from Salem, North Carolina. Holman took over the White estate and soon began to renovate and remodel. Throughout the changes to the house, there remained a hidden staircase in the back that was untouched from the original format of the house. Soon after the renovations were complete, the residents heard strange noises coming from the back stairs. The noise that was heard was unmistakably that of footsteps going up and down—but not normal footsteps. There was the very distinct sound of a footfall, then the unmistakable sound of wood hitting wood. Those who have heard the phantom climber say that the steps are those of a peg-legged man who has not been seen but only heard throughout the years.

The White-Holman House.

Although no one has ever seen a ghost where the footsteps fall, it is assumed that the ghost is that of a man, as the existence of women with peg legs was extremely unusual. Most people think that the spirit must be that of a former slave or servant, who loyally uses the back stairs so as not to disturb the master of the house. The story would be far more interesting if Long John Silver had resided in the house, but alas, he only exists in the imagination of Robert Louis Stevenson.

Hannah's Creek Swamp

As the Civil War came to a close, the people of Georgia and the Carolinas had not only the Union army to worry about but also the raiders who accompanied Sherman's army. After Sherman sacked Atlanta, he decided to rapidly march his army to the sea, cutting all communications and moving as quickly and as unpredictably as possible. To do this, he had to leave his supply trains behind for the most part. During this march, he relied heavily on the units of Union soldiers that were deployed to scavenge the countryside for food and supplies to keep the army moving. These soldiers were given strict instructions, such as to be courteous with the locals and to leave enough for the families to survive. These instructions were quickly abused, and the raiders gained a reputation for cruelty and for taking whatever they wanted.

By the time Sherman entered North Carolina, there were not only the soldiers from the Union army raiding the homes but also bands of common criminals who would masquerade as soldiers to rob and pillage the people of the South. One such group was led by a man named Fanning. His group operated around Smithfield, North Carolina, which is a short distance from Raleigh. His band was particularly ruthless and had a reputation in the area for treachery. One case of the band's brutality was against the Saunders family. Colonel Saunders and his wife were robbed and murdered by the band when they refused to hand over their possessions and allow the group of raiders to violate their home without a fight. After the colonel and his wife were slain, the raiders ransacked the house of all valuables and then burned it to the ground.

A few weeks after the killing of the Saunders family, a young Confederate officer stood before his commanding officer, General Joseph Wheeler, to ask for permission to go after the band. The young officer was the son of Colonel Saunders, and he wanted permission to find the men and make them pay for what they had done. General Wheeler refused to let him go on a ride for vengeance, but he did allow him to take out a group of men to find Fanning. He was to act in a military fashion and leave all personal feelings aside. Saunders set out with his men and tracked the band to an island in Hannah's Creek Swamp. He knew that they could not take the island by force, so they dressed in civilian clothes and posed as another group of raiders to get on the island. Thinking it was a friendly group coming across the water toward the island, Fanning and his men did not take the precaution of arming themselves and found out on the shore the fatal mistake they had made, as the Confederates pulled out their weapons and took all of the men prisoner.

Standing there on the island, Saunders asked who the leader of the band was. Fanning stepped forward defiantly and confidently, thinking that they would be taken to a prison camp and released soon, since the war was drawing to a close. He was surprised when the young Southerner walked up to him and lifted the gold cross from his neck. In the moonlight, it shined as he studied it, remembering the many times he had sat on his mother's lap and looked at the cross the same way. He lifted his eyes to meet Fanning's and introduced himself. The blood left Fanning's face, and he became white as a ghost. Saunders ordered him to be brought with him, and the rest of his band was hanged on the spot there in the swamp. Saunders took Fanning to the burned remains of his family home and hanged him from an oak tree that stood in the family cemetery where his parents rested. Fanning begged in vain for his life that night but to no avail. An eye was taken for an eye that night in 1865.

Today, there is no definite island in the swamp. Nature has changed it to land, but one thing that has not changed since that night is that many people claim to hear the screams and cries of men, begging for their lives, emanating from the swamp. And at night or at dusk, on more than one occasion, people have gone through the swamp and seen, just for a moment, the image of men swinging from ropes on the tall moss-covered trees. Also, at the Saunders family cemetery, many people have heard the begging and crying of a man condemned to death. In both cases, the man's pleas fall on deaf ears, as they did so long ago.

Mill Creek Bridge

Near Smithfield, a legend has been passed down since the 1820s. It is the story of a slave named Old Squire and his master, a man by the name of Lynch. They had gone down by the creek on a sunny day in May to tend to the edge of the cotton field in that area. Master Lynch was not a beloved man, not by his slaves nor by his neighbors. He was a cruel and harsh man who seemed to be waiting at all times for a reason to lash out against anyone. One sunny summer's day, he was extremely agitated by the slow speed at which Old Squire was moving. If there is an opposite for everyone in the world, then Old Squire was Master Lynch's. He was a docile and soft-spoken man who never complained and always tried to bring up the people around him. He was loved both by slaves and whites in the area, who all looked at him as a grandfatherly figure.

Master Lynch rode behind Old Squire on his horse, verbally berating him as he worked. Demanding more and more from him, wanting him to move faster and faster, Old Squire humbly hoed at the ground and stayed to his work, which seemed to agitate Lynch even more. He raised his horsewhip and struck down hard across Old Squire's back. This was not the first time that he had struck Old Squire, but he had never done so in such a sudden manner. Old Squire turned to face his master, and as he did, Lynch raised his hand again and brought down his whip right across Old Squire's face. Enraged, Old Squire instinctively struck back with the hoe that he still held in his hands and watched in horror as Master Lynch fell from his saddle, blood running down the side of his head.

Old Squire knelt down beside Lynch and put his ear to his mouth. He felt no breath; he heard no breathing. Panicked at the thought of what he knew would happen to him when people learned of what had happened, he dragged Master Lynch's body to the soft soil under the bridge over the creek and began to dig. He buried him there and scared the horse away. When he had finished cleaning up the evidence, Old Squire went back to work as if nothing had happened, and he returned to his cabin that night as he usually did. The next day, the search began for the missing Lynch. Old Squire was questioned, along with the other slaves, but he stuck to the story that he had seen Master Lynch that morning on his way out to the field but not since. No one had any reason to suspect a man like Old Squire of murder, so when the master's horse was found wandering through the woods, it was clear to everyone that Master Lynch had crossed the wrong person and that someone had done to him what so many other had wanted to do in the past.

The issue was soon forgotten, as Master Lynch had been a vile man and had made many enemies. His son took over the farm and proved to be a smarter and kinder man than his father had been. Soon after Master Lynch's death, strange things began to happen at the bridge. As people would cross the bridge, they would sometimes hear moaning sounds coming from underneath. Many times, it was reported that at night, if a torch was carried over the bridge, it would go out upon contact with the bridge and would relight on the opposite side. These occurrences were never linked to the death of Master Lynch until the death of Old Squire. He wanted to die with a clear conscience, so on his deathbed he confessed all. After Old Squire joined Master Lynch in the realm of the dead, strange lights were seen dancing around the old bridge over Mill Creek. It is believed that in death, the two men are still fighting it out and will continue to do so for all eternity.

The Devil's Tramping Ground

The location of one of the state's most famous unsolved mysteries is a short distance from Chapel Hill in Siler City, North Carolina. The spot is known as the Devil's Tramping Ground and has become a must-see for paranormal enthusiasts. The legend goes that hundreds of years ago the first settlers in the area came upon a large circle in the forest where nothing would grow. The land was bare and perfectly circular, but outside of the circle, the grass and weeds grew with tall, strong trees. The settlers believed that the Native Americans who had occupied the area long before the settlers arrived had used the grounds for their ceremonies. Dancing for days in the circle, chanting to their gods, had worn the ground down so far that it had rendered the soil useless. Other theories held that the ground was used by the devil himself. He would come there to plan his evil doings and would pace around the circle, stroking his beard, deep in thought. These theories only grew over the years, and as the area grew around the Devil's Tramping Ground, so did its attraction.

People were enthusiastic about the prospects of a place at which true evil could be found. Many people tried to camp on the spot overnight, most to no avail, claiming to have been accosted overnight by Beelzebub himself or just plain feelings of dread that made them flee. Many young men took their sweethearts there for a chance to bring them closer to them and maybe a chance to step in and be a protector to the frightened young lady. As time moved forward, so did the evolution of the myth of the odd circle. During the '60s and '70s, the popular explanation was that aliens had caused the circle by landing there to capture their unwilling subjects.

Over the years, the ground has been tested and found to be sterile, which is the reason that no flora has been able to maintain life there. Also, the circle has also shrunk from the large estimates of the past, and today it is not quite as impressive. It seems that the devil is a raging alcoholic today and leaves his bottles and cans in the ashes of a campfire at the center of the circle. It is hard to find the circle today, but it is right off the road, outside of Siler City.

Bentonville

As the Civil War came to an end, the Union had plans to combine the two great armies in Virginia and destroy the Army of Northern Virginia. General Sherman had paved a path of destruction through the South as he marched to the sea from Atlanta. The Union army held the port of Savannah, and General Grant wanted Sherman to ferry his army by sea to Virginia to combine with his, but Sherman suggested, instead, to drive north through the Carolinas to Goldsboro, where he would link his army with those of Generals Terry and Schofield, who were closing in on Wilmington at the time. Grant trusted Sherman and agreed to his strategy. He led his army north from Savannah through South Carolina with little resistance. Confederate general P.G.T. Beauregard had split the Confederate army between Charleston and Augusta because of the lack of knowledge of Sherman's next move. As Sherman moved through the Carolinas, Robert E. Lee, the Confederate commander, requested that Confederate president Jefferson Davis appoint General Joseph Johnston as commander of all remaining Confederate forces between the Carolinas and Florida. Jefferson Davis was reluctant because he considered Johnston to be a personal enemy, but his faith and trust in Lee overrode his distaste for Johnston, and he made the appointment official.

Johnston quickly began to organize as large a force as he could. He positioned his small army along the road to Goldsboro and waited for Sherman to approach. On March 19, 1865, Johnston attacked the left wing of Sherman's army as it approached Goldsboro. By isolating a smaller force, Johnston had hoped to crush it and move it back into a defensive position, but at the end of the day, they had fought to a tactical draw. The next day, the remainder of Sherman's army arrived, and the battle quickly turned to the Union's favor. After a few more days of skirmishes and defensive actions, Johnston pulled his army back toward Raleigh. On April 26, 1865, he surrendered the remainder of the Confederate forces to General Sherman at Bennett Place, near Durham, North Carolina, bringing the war to a close.

At the battle site today, near the visitor's center and museum, is a two-story white house that served as a hospital during the battle. The house was built about 1855 for John and Amy Harper, who at the time of the battle were living in the house with seven of their nine children. The house was occupied on the first day of fighting by the Union, a place where Union and Confederate alike were cared for and operated on. The Harpers and their children helped the Union medical staff care for these men, and after the battle, when the Union wounded were sent on to Goldsboro, forty-five Confederate wounded remained at the Harper house to receive further treatment and convalesce.

Many people believe that the house is still inhabited by the Harpers. On several occasions, visitors as well as employees have heard heavy footsteps upstairs when no one else is in the house. John Harper has been seen on occasion, standing at the top of the stairs, glaring down at the first floor of his home. Is he looking down on the frightened person who is seeing his ghost, or is his image caught in time, looking down in horror at the carnage that has come into his home?

There have been many reports of the grounds being haunted as well. One famous story that has been retold many times is that of two hunters, living around the turn of the twentieth century, who passed the Harper house in the early morning darkness when they heard the sounds of a battle. Cannons and muskets fired all around them, and they took cover and watched the Battle of Bentonville unfold in front of them one last time. The two men ran from the battle, and days later, when they decided that they were not both crazy, they began to tell the story to anyone who would listen. When they told the story to one old veteran of the battle, he recognized everything. The two men described seeing a young Confederate wrestling with a Union soldier for his unit's colors. Another Confederate soldier ran over to help his comrade, but he was killed with a bayonet strike by a Yankee while coming to help *his* comrade. The old man, with a tear in his eye, said that this was exactly how his brother had died at the battle, coming to his aid to save the colors. The two men were even more spooked than they had been before. Could they have seen the old man's brother being killed so many years ago? Was it a battle of ghosts or a picture in time?

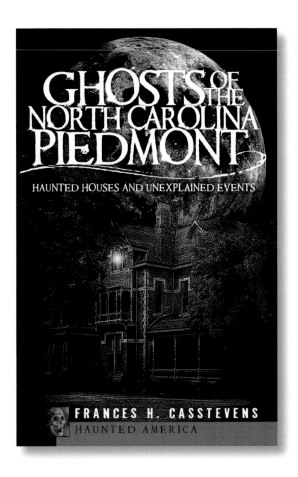

If you enjoyed this book, you may also enjoy Frances H. Cassteven's

GHOSTS OF THE NORTH CAROLINA PIEDMONT

$17.99 • 160 pages • Over 30 images • ISBN 978-1-59629-643-5

The North Carolina Piedmont can be a very spooky place. Whether you believe in ghosts or not, many people in this region have experienced things that simply cannot be explained. This collection of local lore includes classic ghost stories that have been passed down for generations, as well as personal experiences of the author, her family, friends and even strangers. Join local author Frances Casstevens as she recounts one spine-tingling tale after another.

Visit us at
www.historypress.net